Confucius Never Said

CONFUCIUS
NEVER
SAID

Helen Raleigh

ISBN: 9781499185270
Library of Congress Control Number: 2018912384

Chinese Provinces Map
(Society for Anglo-Chinese Understanding)

Figure 1.
1. My father's hometown in Shandong province
2. My mother's hometown in Hubei province
3. My parents were sent by the government to work in the city of Zigong, Sichuan province, which was also the city where I was born.

Forward

In October of 2013, just one week after being sworn in as a new citizen of the United States of America, Helen Raleigh spoke to a packed auditorium of 430 high-school students at Liberty Common High School in Fort Collins, Colorado. The students sat spellbound as they listened to harrowing, first-hand accounts depicting the history of communism in China, and the courageous journey toward the true freedom made possible only by the rational superiority of American capitalism.

Helen's remarks were delivered within the context of the school's Capstone Virtue of Prudence.

"Prudence is about a freeman's ability to make the right decisions based upon reason," she said. "That is why freedom thrives on prudence."

As the principal of Liberty Common High School, I invited Helen to speak because I knew she would be the perfect person to impress upon my students a deeper appreciation for authentic liberty. I had previously witnessed Helen inspire audiences as her story became known among Colorado's most accomplished civic leaders associated with the Leadership Program of the Rockies (LPR).

LPR exists to train up-and-coming leaders to take on a broad array of challenges and problems in the public square. Helen is a member of the LPR Class of 2013. Her classmates and colleagues quickly came to respect her as a fierce advocate for the timeless principles of America's Founding Fathers.

At LPR gatherings, Helen regularly propounded the principle of private property rights as absolutely essential to the maintenance of the Republic. She never missed an opportunity to assert the defense of unalienable individual rights as the only legitimate purpose of government. Ultimately, Helen was awarded LPR's prestigious "Defender of Capitalism Award"—a highly competitive and revered title involving a written essay and an oral defense before a panel of economists and scholars.

As the chairman of LPR, I regard Helen's forceful, consistent, and courageous defense of capitalism as a postulate that ought to be heard and considered by every American. It is persuasive because it is personal. It is authoritative because it is a veritable rendition of self-evident truths.

Helen asked the Liberty Common High School students, "How would you feel if I tell you that I don't trust you to make the right decisions, so I will make all the decisions for you? I will tell you how much you can eat, what you should major in in college, who you will have to work for, and where you have to live."

Many of the youngsters must have wondered at that moment whether these questions were rhetorical. "You must think I'm being ridiculous," she continued, "but that was exactly what happened to my father."

As with most epic Chinese stories, Helen's draws upon the experience of a family spanning multiple generations. It traces a cycle of tranquility to bondage, from bondage to a dreadful struggle, from struggle to prosperity, and from there to glorious tranquility again. This grand story, complete with lessons of timeless economic truths, is beautifully told upon each page of *Confucius Never Said*.

The personal qualities of Helen's story reveal classical confirmations about human nature and anthropological responses to economic and political conditions. Her family members' love for one another, and their unyielding adherence to universal virtues, frames each character with seemingly superhuman strength.

In *Confucius Never Said*, Helen takes appropriately bold advantage of her immigrant station and her fresh citizenship. Her story reminds us all of why capitalism and republicanism have, for centuries, attracted freedom seekers to American shores. Hers is one more credible and powerful example of how rugged individualism and gritty self-determination secure the American Dream.

China's history is directly relevant to America today. Not only does the future of China have a close bearing upon the future of the United States, but its communist trappings are too painful to be ignored. Bereft of true property rights, true justice, and true individual rights, China proves today how the objectives of collectivism are inevitably achieved by force, through violence, and through the dehumanizing treatment of regular people.

Helen underscores these lessons clearly and vividly throughout her book. She proposes the cardinal virtue of prudence as the antidote to both bureaucracy and its penchant for central control. Her story makes an airtight case for virtuous leadership suffused in moral philosophy.

Confucius Never Said contrasts the power and importance of the individual with the weakness and cruelty of the soulless, collective whole that defines both past and modern communism.

As Helen finished her presentation to the young American citizens assembled at Liberty Common High School, she assured them, "As long as you have a solid set of virtues and moral principles guiding you like the North Star, you will never get lost in the dark."

The inspiring saga of Helen's family casts an intense floodlight upon the hideous depths of Chinese communism. The reader is then redirected upward along a path toward the commanding heights of liberty. It is only within the bright embrace of American-style liberty that we can so easily agree upon the timeless principle that "all men are created equal."

With sweet irony, Helen traces her family's past to the same Chinese province that is also the birthplace of Confucius himself in 551 BC. For all the brilliance and genius attributed to this venerable Chinese philosopher, it is Confucius who failed to discover this most important self-evident truth upon which America's Founding Fathers built the freest political and economic system in the history of human civilization.

Indeed, by their own declaration of this self-evident, universal truth of human equality, revolutionary Americans set themselves free, thereby launching a rebirth of genuine liberty set upon the high virtue of prudence. This is the torch of freedom which the Founders held up for themselves, for their countrymen, for their posterity, for Helen Raleigh, and for all those who are blessed to know her remarkable story.

Bob Schaffer
Principal, Liberty Common High School, Fort Collins, Colorado
Chairman, Leadership Program of the Rockies
Member of Congress (1997-2003)

Reflections on *Confucius Never Said*

As I read the manuscript of this book by my friend Helen Raleigh, two powerful reactions gripped me simultaneously. One was horror at what her parents and grandparents witnessed under Chinese communism. The other was gratitude to Helen for sharing their story.

There is a bittersweet irony here. In keeping with Mao's insane goal to wipe out the past, a communist functionary destroyed the genealogy book that had documented centuries of Helen's ancestors. Now, by painstakingly reconstructing the history of her family's last four generations, Helen is putting her homeland's tormentors on notice: Things like family, conscience, character and truth matter immensely—and are far more permanent than the destructive fantasies of men who briefly wield great power.

Maximilien Robespierre, architect of the French Revolution's "Reign of Terror," is said to have justified mass murder by declaring that "to make an omelet, one must break eggs." Like all ruthless, power-mad ideologues before and since—including Mao Zedong—Robespierre never made an omelet. He only broke eggs. Mao did it by the millions. While pseudo-intellectuals of the American and European Left ignored his crimes or even applauded them, Mao perpetrated theft, misery and death on a scale virtually without precedent. Helen Raleigh doesn't need another lecture on communism because she knows how her family suffered it firsthand. And she's wise enough to understand that its kissing cousin, socialism, is also a scourge to avoid.

From its first page, this is a deeply personal story. It's undoubtedly one that Helen has desired to tell for many years. It couldn't have been an easy task. There are so many things she and her family saw and heard that most people would want to forget. But Helen is not one to let tyrants off the hook. Through the story of her family, she wants the world to know what millions of people endured as victims of a radical social experiment. She wants us all to comprehend its meaning and its relevance to our day. She wants us to appreciate the freedoms we still have in America and work to restore the ones we've lost.

The great strength of this book comes at the end of each chapter under the heading, "Food for Thought." It is in those few paragraphs that the author sharpens the focus and distills the lessons from her family's experience: Men bent on power will make promises they have no intention or ability to keep. Truth is the first casualty of power, followed by a growing body count. Private property is a human right and assaults on it degrade and destroy humanity. Don't be suckered by demagogues who pit class against class and demonize those who stand in their way. Freedom is worth fighting for and living for because without it, life is unthinkable. Never give up on what you know to be right, no matter what established authority or the temper of the times may dictate.

My friendship with the author is a recent one and yet now that I know her family's story, I feel as though I have known her for decades. She fights for something her friends and family members were denied. Like so many unsung heroes of history, she is a passionate defender of that noblest of earthly ideals — human liberty.

Thank you, Helen Raleigh, for giving us this book!

Lawrence W. Reed

President

Foundation for Economic Education, www.fee.org

April 2011

CHAPTER 1

A Landlord's Fate

My great-grandfather's final wish was to be buried with his ancestors on land that had been cultivated by the family for generations. His final wish was never granted. The reason why can give us much food for thought.

My great-grandfather was born in 1900 in a village called Qiu, which is located in Shandong province on the east coast of China. Shandong province is renowned for two seemingly contradictory things: philosophy and banditry.

The first is philosophy. Shandong province is the home of Confucius (551–479 BC), a great teacher and philosopher who established the system of morality and proper conduct that dominated China for more than 2000 years. His teachings influenced generations of Chinese on how to live their lives and interact with others, and on the forms of society and government in which they should participate. Confucius established strict social orders of respect and obedience for Chinese society. For instance, Confucius believed people should obey and respect their ruler just as they obey and respect their fathers, while a ruler should love and care for his subjects as if they were his children. Confucius believed that harmony in society can only be achieved when every man perform his own social responsibility within his destined social orders. Because of his wisdom and influence, Confucius sometimes was called the Socrates of the East.

In ancient China, any male who wished to serve at the imperial court had to take the imperial examination, which was based on Confucius's philosophy. Those who passed the exam were said to bring great honors to their families. That was probably why my great-grandfather was given a very poetic name. His middle name was Dian (殿), which means *palace*, and his first name was Wen (文), which means *literature*. Maybe his father had high hopes that he would one day pass the imperial examination and become a government official.

The second thing Shandong province is famous for is banditry. Though people of Shandong are particularly mindful of Confucius's teachings of obedience and respect authorities, Shandong province is known as the stronghold of the 108 legendary bandits who rebelled against the government during the Song Dynasty (960-1279 AD). These bandits preyed upon the rich and became known as the "righteous bandits" — or, as I call them, the "Robin Hoods of China." Their legends were glorified in the classical Chinese novel *Water Margin*.

Since banditry had been prevalent in Shandong province for many centuries, many local people, including my great-grandfather, practiced martial arts to protect themselves and their families. The people of Shandong are known throughout China as people who are normally well mannered but should never be underestimated.

The Qiu village where my great-grandfather lived had about 200 people making up 50 households. A main street (which was just a dirt road) divided the village into north and south sides. On the south side lived the Qiu clan, after whom the village was named. On the north side lived the Zhou clan, including my great-grandfather.

Zhou is a significant family name in China. Legend says it comes from the Zhou dynasty (1046-256 BC). Through thousands of years' movement, Zhou clan members have become scattered around China. Because our particular branch of the Zhou clan has lived in Qiu village for 50 generations, I joke with my American husband that I am a Chinese princess with a royal family name.

Though my great-grandfather had a very poetic name and received a typical education in Confucian teaching, he didn't end up serving at China's imperial court. The imperial court ceased to exist when the last emperor of Qin dynasty was forced by rebels to abdicate on February 12, 1912. Therefore, my great-grandfather became a wheat farmer.

Being a farmer in 1900s in China was a tough way of making a living. Since very few machines were used, farming was mostly done by hand. My great-grandfather sweated on every inch of the land near where his ancestors were buried. Because of his hard work, he was able to accumulate some land in addition to what he had inherited from his father. He expected that someday he would be buried near his ancestors, while his children and grandchildren continued to plow his land.[1]

Land to a Chinese farmer is more important than life itself. That is why the Chinese Communist Party pushed for "land reform" as soon as they took over China in 1949: to win the support of China's 300 million peasants .

To set the stage for the land reform, the Communists introduced a class system in each village. The class system, closely followed the Soviet Union's classification model, and became the basis for land reform. Then, in 1950, Chairman Mao Zedong passed the Agrarian Reform Law. Work teams made up of communist party members were sent to villages in order to assign each villager to one of the five classes: landlord, rich peasant, middle peasant, poor peasant, and laborer.

A work team made up of one woman and two men came to my great-grandfather's village. They were Communist Party members. They first divided the villagers into two camps: those who owned land and those who owned no land. Villagers who were landless were either assigned to the laborer class or the poor peasant class. These two classes of villagers were members of the rural proletariats. The work team relied on the help of these rural proletariats to arbitrarily designate other villagers as landlords, rich peasants, and middle peasants.

Because the work team came with a mandated quota, a certain percentage of villagers had to be designated as landlords and rich peasants, despite the fact that many farmers in the villages shared similar economic conditions. Initially, some poor farmers were hesitant to identify their neighbors as rich. However, the work team brainwashed the poor farmers into believing that disproportionate property ownership was the main cause of social injustice and that landowners were evil class enemies and exploiters of the poor. With a certain amount of coercion, some poor farmers turned their old grievances or frustrations into hatred for their well-to-do neighbors. Since my great-grandfather owned land, he was

---

[1] If you want to know what land means to a Chinese farmer, I would highly recommend reading Pearl Buck's wonderful book *The Good Earth*.

classified as a landlord even though he wasn't the richest man in the village.

After everyone in the village was assigned to a class, the work team organized a number of "speak bitterness" meetings. During those meetings, poor peasants and laborers were encouraged to vent their frustration against the landlord and rich peasant classes. Initially, villagers were hesitant to speak ill of someone in public, especially someone they were related to. This kind of public demonstration of hatred was against their Confucian teachings, because the core of Confucianism emphasizes that people should be respectful, loyal, and kind towards one another.

But the work team members were good at turning people against one another. Envy and greed were powerful tools in inflaming hatred and resentment towards any villagers who owned property. My great-grandfather often had to stand in front of the village crowd, with his head bent, listening to his neighbors and relatives accuse him of many wrongdoings that were either grossly exaggerated or plain false. One of his relatives even came up to him and spat in his face. I can't imagine what went through his mind during this, or how he survived the humiliation.

Similar and even worse things were taking place throughout China. Most landlords and rich farmers were rounded up and were either executed or sent to labor camps. Local governments confiscated their belongings—such as cattle and land—and redistributed them to landless and impoverished farmers.

My great-grandfather's life was spared, and he didn't have to go to the labor camp because none of his clan members had the guts to send him. Yet his relatives and other poor neighbors didn't hesitate to take his land, cattle, and even farming tools away from him. The government was able to successfully inflame such envy and hatred in poor people toward the rich people that nobody felt sorry about taking a rich man's property. My great-grandfather saw himself turned from a rich farmer into a poor farmer overnight. A once closely-knit village became a place where a class system was clearly defined and a new group of haves and have-nots existed.

By the end of 1951, over 10 million former landowners' properties had been expropriated[2] and over 700 million *mu* of land (115 million acres) and various means of production were redistributed among 300 million formerly landless farmers. [3] Nobody knows for sure how many landowners were killed in the land reform. It was said that locals were given quotas of how many landlords had to be identified, denounced, and killed per village. Not even the landlords' children were spared this terrible fate. It is estimated the total number of people who were killed from 1947 to 1952 was one to two million.[4] The so-called land reform was nothing more than calculated terrorism in the name of wealth redistribution.

It was said that people who carried out this kind of violence displayed fanatical convictions. They truly believed that they did it to achieve the greater good of the society. Their blind faith enabled them to believe that murdering a group of minorities (in this case, determined by property ownership) was the right price to pay for a better society, one that proclaimed equality, justice, and freedom.

The poor farmers didn't get the long end of the stick either. In 1953, three years after the land reform, the Chinese government announced an agricultural collectivization movement. This mandatory process was introduced incrementally. First, farmers were organized into "mutual help teams." Farmers within each mutual help team were forced to share tools and cattle. The concept of what was "yours" vs. "mine" was replaced by what was "ours." These teams were gradually merged into cooperatives, and later these cooperatives would be merged into large "people's communes." In each commune, everything was shared. Village women were told by their village leaders that individual household cooking was banned, so their private kitchens became obsolete. Everyone ate at the commune cafeteria. Enormous food waste was prevalent, which wasn't surprising. Why should people be frugal when they could feast on a seemingly unlimited supply of free food?

Throughout the collectivization process, the land that had been handed out to the poor farmers was gradually returned to the state. By

---

[2] Dikotter, 2013
[3] Land Reform and Collectivization (1950-1953)
[4] Dikotter, 2013

1958, there was no private land ownership.   Private farming was prohibited, and anyone who engaged in it was labeled as a counter revolutionary and persecuted. Farmers were required to sell their produce to the government; no private sales were allowed. Farmers couldn't decide for themselves what crops to grow. Instead, they had to follow the orders of the local communist leaders.   Unfortunately, many local communist leaders didn't know much about farming, so the orders they issued were unwise and the results were disastrous.

Farmers had a rude awakening when they realized that helping the government expropriate property from "rich" people meant they were basically giving the government carte blanche to ignore property rights. They also realized that what government gives you, the government can take away.

In Guangdong province, discontented farmers sang the following song:[5]

Collectivization, collectivization,
Nobody earns, somebody spends,
Members eat but teams spend,
Teams earn but brigades spend
Brigades eat but communes spend.

This kind of song showed the damage done to the motivation of farmers by the collectivization policies. Sure enough, people who were caught singing this kind of song were persecuted by their local governments.

The Chinese collectivization movement was modeled after the Soviet Union's agricultural collectivization movement, which took place from 1929 to 1933.   The immediate result of the Soviet's collectivization movement was a famine from 1932 to 1933 in the major grain producing parts of the country (such as Ukraine). Calculations based on the Soviet archives put the deaths at three to four million people[6]. Mao liked to brag that he was a fervent student of history. Apparently, he failed to learn the lessons of the Soviet' collectivization experience. Notwithstanding the

---

[5] Dikötter, 2010
[6] Fitzpatrick, 1994

mounting historical evidence, he pushed the collectivization in China with zeal and treated ordinary Chinese people's lives as expendable. As with the Soviet's experience, a famine resulted. The Great Chinese Famine took place from 1959 to 1961. During it, an estimated 30 to 60 million Chinese people perished[7]. As George Santayana famously said, "Those who cannot remember the past are condemned to repeat it."

My great-grandfather was lucky. He wasn't among the one million landowners who were executed during the land reform. He also survived the Famine, even though many of his family members and relatives didn't. I have no way of knowing how my great-grandfather felt about these ordeals. The first time I met him, he was already in his 80s, and I was only eight. I can guess now that these losses brought him endless sorrow, but in my memory, he never showed any despair. He always walked tall and with dignity. Years later, when I learned the phrase "Bent, but not broken," I thought of my great-grandfather.

My great-grandfather never talked much about love, but he showed his love and affection by his actions. For example, the main diet in my village was flour-based because almost everyone was a wheat farmer. Every morning, my grandma would make steamed buns for breakfast. Most of the buns were brown because they were made out of what today I would call "whole wheat." ("Whole" meaning all of the grain was used; nothing was lost in the process of making the flour.) In the bamboo steamer, there were always two white buns. They were made from refined flour. They were specially prepared for my great-grandfather, because buns made from refined flour were easier to chew for an old man like him. But we all knew white buns also tasted so much better than brown ones. I couldn't help asking my grandma once, "Why can't we all eat white buns?" She answered only by gently stroking my hair while trying to hold her tears back. Later, my cousin told me that refined flour was much more expensive than whole wheat flour. Only Great-Grandfather could enjoy this special treatment, because he was old. But apparently, Great-Grandfather didn't enjoy being treated differently. He always waited till grandma turned around before sneaking the white buns to my cousin and me. I couldn't understand at my young age why wheat farmers couldn't

---

[7] Dikötter, 2010

afford to eat the refined flour they produced. Nowadays, when I am willing to pay more for whole wheat bread than for white bread, I can't help but wonder what my great-grandfather would think.

My great-grandfather never stopped farming, even though he didn't hold any deed to claim the land that had been originally his. He continued to give it all he had. He went to the field every day until the day he passed away. His final wish was to be buried with his ancestors. However, after the communists took over China, families were not allowed to bury their family members in their ancestral graves anymore because all lands belonged to the people—which meant they really belonged to the government. Family burial plots were considered a bad feudalist practice. Instead, the village designated a public burial place that was far from our village. Our ancestral grave plot had been turned into farmland and could no longer be located, so my great-grandfather's final wish was never granted.

Food for Thought

The history of China's "land reform" was written in the tears and blood of landowners like my great-grandfather. But the 300 million poor Chinese farmers were victims too. They gave the Communist Party their popular support, hoping to improve their living standards by taking property away from landowners. Instead, they became stepping stones for the Party to abolish private property rights once and for all.

Despite these historical facts, "make the rich pay" has never lost its popular appeal. We've all heard arguments like this: "If you are rich, it doesn't hurt to pay a little more." But who has the authority to define how much more is enough? Who can determine what hurts and what doesn't? If we remain silent or even encourage our government to violate one group's property rights for another group's benefit, like those poor Chinese farmers did, what will stop the government from violating *our* property rights?

It is worth noting that honoring private property rights protects not just the rich; it especially protects the poor. In his famed book *The Road to Serfdom*, Friedrich Hayek called property rights "the most important guarantee of freedom. . . . It is only because the control of the means of production is divided among many people acting independently that nobody has complete power over us, that we as individuals can decide what to do with ourselves." That is why the founders of the United States were so insistent on recognizing and protecting private property rights in this land of the free.

Ultimately, the right to property is about the right to act. With property rights protection, an individual feels a sense of ownership about his future. He is motivated to study, save, work, and take risks as he sees fit. Without property rights, there is no individual freedom and no incentive to work hard. Eventually, the standard of living will go down for all, but as Chinese history has shown the poor will suffer most.

Assaults on property rights are driven by envy. But one of the reasons America is the richest country in the world is that American culture is about aspirations, not envy. In later chapters, I will share with you my personal journey, which gave me confidence that each one of us can live a better life if we choose to live it by our own efforts.

CHAPTER 2

The Landlord's Grandson

My father often said that he had two childhoods. What he really meant was that he had very different childhood memories before and after 1949. The Chinese Communist Party took over China in 1949, when he was nine years old. After he witnessed his family's properties being confiscated by village leaders and redistributed to everyone else, he knew that his worry-free childhood was over.

When I asked him what his favorite childhood memories were, he always went back to the good times before 1949. He told me his favorite time was of course Chinese New Year, which was the most important traditional Chinese holiday. Chinese New Year celebrations traditionally started on Chinese New Year's Eve and ended with the Lantern Festival, which fell on the 15th day of the first month, making the festival the longest on the Chinese calendar. Because the Chinese calendar is lunar based, Chinese New Year is also referred to as the Lunar New Year. Since Chinese New Year is a holiday centered on the family, it is celebrated in countries and regions with Chinese populations. Just like Thanksgiving in the U.S., people in China will travel miles to be with their families on Chinese New Year and feast on many delicious foods. My father told me that his favorite Chinese New Year dish was Jiaozi, Chinese dumplings.

Dumplings have been part of Chinese food culture for a long time. Its history can be traced all the way to the Song Dynasty (960-1279). Dumplings are not an everyday food. Chinese people eat dumplings only on special occasions, such as on Chinese New Year or before a loved one leaves for a trip. These crescent-shaped dumplings with pleated edges are normally filled with pork and leeks. One could tell a household's wealth by the proportion of pork versus leeks inside a dumpling. The filling ingredients are enclosed in flour-based dough that is thicker than a wonton wrapper. A traditional custom is to put something special inside one of the dumplings. Whoever eats the dumpling with the special fillings is said to be a lucky person who will have good fortune in the coming year. Some families will make a dumpling filled with candy. In my family, my grandmother would fill one dumpling with coins.

Figure 2. Chinese Dumplings

Besides food, Chinese New Year celebrations were full of traditional rituals, which were passed on from one generation to the next. On the Chinese New Year's Eve, my great-grandfather would put the family genealogy book on display in the center of the living room. A genealogy book (家谱) was the most valuable possession of a traditional Chinese family. Many families and clans have **genealogy records** that extended over several hundred years or more. It is generally accepted that the longest continuous Chinese genealogy record belongs to descendants of Confucius. Traditionally, even though every family member was included in the book, only males' full names were recorded. Women would be recorded in the genealogy book only by their family names. When a woman got married, her name would be crossed out of her family's genealogy book and be entered in her in-law's family genealogy book with her in-law's family name in front of her maiden name.

My father told me that the Zhou clan's genealogy book covered our entire 50 generations. Like other traditional genealogy books, it contained a generation poem. The poem had four lines, with five words in each line. The tradition was to use one word from the poem as the middle name for each generation. For example, all my great-grandfather's generation shared the same middle name—Dian (殿), which means *palace*. My father's generation shared the middle name Yu (玉), which means *jade*. After all the words in the generation poem were used, the next generation would start from the first word of the poem again. For a big clan like ours, it was not someone's age but his middle name that told us his seniority. Our genealogy book was our closest connection to our ancestors. It also functioned like a thread: No matter where a clan member lived, he was always connected with his family through the genealogy book. The worst disgrace for a Chinese person, especially a man, was to be eliminated from his family genealogy book. It meant he was rootless and had no ties to anyone.

Because the genealogy book played such an important role in our family, Great-grandfather only put it on display once a year, on Chinese New Year. Next to the genealogy book, in the center of the room, fruit and meat dishes were served. Nobody was allowed to touch these dishes, because they were meant for our ancestors. Since my father was the first born grandson of the family, my great-grandfather normally took him to visit our ancestral tombs and burn incense. My father would bend his knees and bow to our ancestral tombs, while great-grandfather invited our ancestors to come home for the New Year's feast. Afterwards, Great-Grandfather and my father would return home and wait. This was the time that everyone had to be careful. No one was allowed to speak loudly or cry because it could disturb our ancestors' spirits while they enjoyed the feast. If someone cried, it was considered a bad omen.

On New Year's Day, everyone got up before dawn. My father and the other children lit firecrackers to welcome the New Year and drive away evil spirits. My grandma cooked dumplings. After everyone finished eating dumplings, the kids would begin an activity called Bai Nian, which meant they knelt down and bowed. They first bowed down to our ancestors, then to the most senior people of our families, and then to the extended families, relatives, and so on. In return, kids always received Hong Bao—money wrapped up in red paper, red being considered a good luck color in China. The day after the New Year's Day, everyone would bow to our genealogy book and light firecrackers to send our ancestors' spirits away. Afterwards, my great-grandfather would put the genealogy book away, because on the third day of the New Year, it was customary for in-laws to visit, and it was considered bad luck to let anyone outside your direct family see your genealogy book.

Every time my father talked about these good old days before 1949, his face lit up as if he was reliving those happy moments.

"What happened after 1949?" I asked him.

He shook his head and told me that many customs were banned because Mao decided that, in order to build a new Communist China, Chinese people had to destroy the Four Olds — old ideas, old cultures, old customs, and old habits. This kind of obliteration broke the traditional family and community bonds. Our family genealogy book, which had survived hundreds of years of dynasty changes, wars, and floods, didn't survive Mao's movement. A young and overzealous clan member threw our genealogy book into fire, along with other antiques. Information about our ancestors was lost forever. Ever since, the Zhou clan has been living like a tree without roots. My father explained to me that that was why neither my siblings nor I had middle names: no one remembered the generation poem from the genealogy book. The loss of that book brings him endless sorrow even today.

After the government's land reform from 1949–1951, my father's life was turned upside down. He witnessed the disappearance of our family's fortune through government-sanctioned redistribution. He rarely had enough to eat. He learned that no matter how hard his grandparents and parents worked in the field, they couldn't lay claim to the fruits of their labor. In fact, they were no longer farmers; they were agricultural workers. They received work points by following the orders of village leaders. Food was distributed to each household based on the work points household members earned.

After the land reform, farmers were required to sell their produce only to the government and only at a fixed price. Private transactions were strictly forbidden, so farmers had no other income source. My grandfather used to sell baby clothing in winter to supplement his income until he had to stop because a village leader warned him that commercial success meant he was exploiting the poor.

The Chinese government proclaimed that being poor was "glorious." However, many people didn't share that sentiment. People were just afraid to be called "rich" because they had witnessed the ruthless persecution of "landlords" and "rich farmers." People stopped working hard because no one wanted to rise above his neighbors. In any case, it didn't matter whether anyone worked hard or not. As long a person showed up in the field, he would receive the same amount of food as the next person.

Since fewer people were willing to work hard, production went down dramatically. At the same time, the government requisition of grain kept going up, especially during the Korean War period (25 June 1950–27 July 1953). In 1950, Chinese people were told that the South Koreans, aided by the American imperialists, had attacked the peaceful North Koreans with the goal of invading China. (This is how the Korean War is taught to Chinese schoolchildren even today.) Young men like my father's older cousins were forcefully drafted into the "volunteer army." Government procurement of everything from grain to cotton went up sharply. With lower production, higher procurement, and a lower labor force, farmers had very little left to support themselves and their families. According to historical records, by 1954, five years after the Communist Party liberated China, Chinese farmers had a third less food to eat than before liberation[8].

An adolescent American boy probably spends most of his time worrying about girls. My father spent his adolescent years worrying about two things: Where to find food and how to pay his junior high school tuition. Tuition in the 1950s was very inexpensive by any standard. Each semester, tuition plus books cost only ten yuan (a little over one dollar). In those years, a school day started at eight a.m. and went all day except for a lunch break. Students were also required to do 90 minutes of evening study at school. Therefore, a school day ended at eight p.m. The middle school my father attended provided a monthly meal plan to cover daily lunch and dinner. The meal plan cost only six yuan (not even one dollar) per month. Yet his parents and grandparents always struggled to come up with even that small amount of money. So he opted out of the school's meal plan to save money. Instead, he brought a bun from home every morning, and he ate half for lunch and half for dinner.

My father was very self-conscious about his lack of means, so he always stayed behind in the classroom when everyone else left for the cafeteria. One day, his biology instructor, Mr. Sun, invited him to have dinner with him. My father was embarrassed to say that he had no money

---

[8] Dikötter, 2013

and could not buy food.

"Don't worry about it." Teacher Sun patted his shoulder and took him to the teachers' cafeteria. There were no tables and chairs in the teachers' cafeteria. People bought food there, put it in their lunch boxes, and went back to eat in their dorms. Teacher Sun bought my father two buns, a bowl of green bean porridge, and a small dish of pickled radish. He put his lunch box on the floor. Teacher Sun and my father squatted down and started eating. Teacher Sun didn't eat much. He was mostly watching my father, who swallowed everything as quickly as he could, since he was hungry and didn't care about his table manners that much. After he finished, Teacher Sun patted his shoulder again and reminded him to go back to the classroom for evening study. Everyone was on food quota then, so my father was pretty sure that he had eaten what should have been Teacher Sun's daily food allocation. Teacher Sun would have to go on being hungry for the rest of that day. Years later, when I asked my father what the best meal he ever had was, he recalled this meal provided by Teacher Sun. "I tried to track him down many years later so I could thank him," my father said, "but people told me that he died during the Great Chinese Famine in 1961. Why do bad things always happened to good people?"

With a constantly half-empty stomach, my father completed junior high in 1957. He didn't have cakes and balloons to celebrate this important milestone in his young life. His family couldn't support him to go to high school. He didn't dare dream about going to college. As the grandson of a landlord, his only choices were: become a solider or become a farmer. In the end, he went home to become a farmer.

My father's life as a farmer didn't last long. In November 1957, communist leaders from around the world gathered in Moscow to celebrate the 40th anniversary of the October Revolution. The Soviet leader Khrushchev announced that his country's goal was to exceed the United States in industrial output in the next fifteen years. Mao Zedong didn't want to be outdone, so he boasted that China's objective was to catch up with and surpass the United Kingdom in steel output in less than fifteen years. To back up his promise, Mao launched the Great Leap Forward movement in 1958, with the goal of turning China from an agricultural society into a communist industrial powerhouse through industrialization and collectivization. Mao and his radical comrades believed that as long as they had the willpower and an abundant supply of cheap labor, they could ignore the laws of nature and economics.

The Communist Party launched a mass steel campaign. Everywhere in China, including the small village where my father lived, people built small backyard furnaces, attempting to produce steel. Every village had a quota to meet. Everyone from eight-year-old kids to eighty-year-old seniors pitched in on around-the-clock shifts by the back yard furnaces.

Few farmers had any energy left to pay attention to what was going on

**Figure 3. Backyard furnaces during Mao's steel campaign in 1958
(Wikipedia Common)**

in the fields. To keep the furnaces burning all day every day, people threw anything they could find into the furnace: coal, wood, dry grass, and dried cow manure. Anything that contained metal, including farming tools and cooking pots, was smashed and fed into the furnaces. However, all these efforts yielded useless return. No steel, but only pig iron, was produced. This high-carbon pig iron had to be decarbonized to make steel. But that was a process a backyard furnace couldn't handle. Therefore, everyone's effort turned out to be worthless.

When the village leaders asked my grandparents to donate any household items containing metal, my grandma naively asked them if she could at least keep a cooking pot. The village leaders laughed at her first and then told her that she didn't have to cook anymore. As a matter of fact, private kitchens were not allowed. Instead, all villagers ate together for free at the cafeteria of the newly formed People's Commune. They were told that this was what Communist society looked like.

One day in June 1958, village leaders issued a new order: males aged between eighteen and sixty had to take part in building a water conservancy construction project. Nobody was allowed to go home, and everybody had to eat and sleep on the construction site. My father was a couple of months away from turning eighteen, but the village head decided he was old enough to contribute to this great project. He had to carry heavy soil in baskets balanced on a shoulder-pole. Like everyone else, the only solid food he got was a steamed bun for lunch. For breakfast and dinner, very watered-down porridge was served. There was so little rice in the porridge that people joked that they could wash their face with the porridge.

While most of the village men were occupied at the construction site, produce rotted in the fields. Despite this, local communist leaders, who were afraid to be accused of being laggards, pressured farmers to exceed an already unrealistic grain production quota. With no choice, village leaders used the previous years' grain reserve and even the next year's seeds to fake a harvest. These were the disastrous policies from central to local governments that caused the Famine a year later.

The year 1958 saw my father hit the lowest point of his young life. As the grandson of a landlord, he saw no hope in his future. But as the old saying goes, "When God closes a door, he opens a window." One day, out of exhaustion and hunger, he passed out at the worksite. When he woke up, he decided that he had to do something to change his life. Coincidentally, one of his former classmates from the junior high stopped by the construction site and told him that an electrical vocation school in Beijing was recruiting students. If he was accepted, the school would cover his room, board, and tuition.

My father couldn't just pack up and leave. He had to get permission from two team captains. The captain who shared his family name said no. Fortunately, the other captain, Mr. Qiu, had some conscience. He said something that my father would be grateful for for the rest of his life. He said to Captain Zhou: "This kid has always been a good student. If he succeeds, he could go to school in Beijing, our great capital. It will be a great honor for our village. We should let him go." Captain Zhou still hesitated. Before he could utter another "No," my father ran back to his mud shed, packed the few belongings he had, and left with his friend.

While my father and his friend waited to catch a train to Beijing, he was painfully aware that he had no money on him. At that moment, he saw one of his aunts, who worked at the local hospital, passing by the train station. When she learned that my father wanted to go to school in Beijing, she was very supportive. She emptied her pocket and gave him five yuan. That was all the money she had. She also gave him her pen and a notebook. My father had been penniless several hours ago, but now he had five yuan in his pocket. He felt like he was dreaming. He was so overjoyed that he didn't even remember to ask his aunt how she was going to get herself home without any money. Another thing he didn't realize then was that this would be the last time he would see his aunt. Two years later, during the Famine, she starved to death. Out of her family of five people, four of them died of hunger. Only one of her sons survived.

At the train station, my father couldn't possibly foresee what was going to take place. For the moment, he sensed that his life was about to change. He bought a platform ticket for five cents and sneaked onto a train to Beijing with his friend. After he arrived at Beijing Railway Station, he quickly realized that five yuan wouldn't last him very long in a big city like Beijing. Fortunately, the recruiting staff from the Beijing Industrial School set up a booth right outside the Beijing train station. After learning about my father's situation, the staff suggested that he talk to their vice principal, Mr. Feng. Principal Feng was a very kind person. He asked my father a few questions and told him not to worry. Then he asked a staff member to take my father and his friends to the school and give them some meal tickets. He also instructed the staff to find an empty classroom so the boys could spend the night.

My father didn't join his friend to eat at the school cafeteria. The entrance exam wouldn't take place until twelve days later, so he needed to plan his food budget wisely to survive till then. Every day, he spent only ten cents for one meal. His daily meal was always the same: two pancakes made out of corn flour and a small pickled radish. Whenever he was thirsty, he drank from the faucet. He didn't have a water cup or a wash towel. Whenever he needed to wash his face, he got some cold water from the faucet and splashed it onto his face. He didn't care much about his living conditions. He was blissful because, for the first time in his life, he was about to take charge of his own destiny.

Later, he passed the exam easily and was admitted to the chemical school. A couple of years later, the Beijing Government combined several vocational schools into Beijing Industrial University, and my father became the first university student from his village.

Figure 4. My father with his classmates in Beijing. He is second to the left in the front row.

Many years later I asked my father, "Have you ever worried that things may not work out? What if you never met your aunt or you never met Mr. Feng?" He told me: "Of course I worried about those things. But what's my choice? Be like a fish lying on the chopping board and let others decide whatever they want to do to me? This alternative was so unbearable that I was determined to find a way out, no matter how hard it would be."

My father's gutsy move not only changed his life forever, it also saved it.

Food for Thought

The kind of poverty and subsistence living that my father and millions of other Chinese people grew up with was a direct result of the poor policies driven by the government's overzealous push for economic equality through command and control. Yet the only thing Chinese people equally shared was misery.

Instead of suffering and obeying, my father chose to do whatever it took to change his fate. James Russell Lowell once said, "Fate loves the fearless." If not for my father's determined mind and gutsy action, he probably would not have escaped the fate of being a farmer, and he may not have survived the Famine. Without a doubt, he couldn't have accomplished his transition without the kindness of others, such as Teacher Sun and my father's aunt. Even a small act of kindness helps preserve our humanity in the most difficult circumstance.

On the other hand, my father's struggle also shows that in a totalitarian regime, no matter how much an individual yearns to take control of his own fate, what he can do is limited.

Unlike my father and millions of Chinese, everyone in America—every man, woman and child, whether rich or poor— has the freedom to choose, freedom to shape his or her own destiny. Don't you agree that you can better manage your own life than other people can?

Therefore, it puzzles me to see more and more Americans today willingly give up control of their lives in exchange for government entitlements. Today's welfare state has built a culture of dependency with ever more people relying on a growing federal government for support. The U.S. Government plays the caregiver role that used to be held by individuals, families, neighborhoods, churches, and other civil society institutions—and it does so by spending other people's money inefficiently and ineffectively. Many people who grow up in this environment don't realize that government assistance comes with two notable costs: the unfair cost to those whose wealth is confiscated to support the government programs and the cost to those on the receiving end who pay by giving up freedom and dignity. Does this sound like a fair trade to you?

CHAPTER 3

From Bad to the Worst

When people welcomed the Communist Party in 1949, they believed that they ushered in the new era the Party promised: freedom and economic equality for all. It didn't take very long for them to realize that those promises couldn't be further from the truth.

1949 to 1959 saw at least 10 different campaigns launched by Mao and his zealous communist comrades. These political campaigns served two main objectives: first, to completely transform China into a communist, utopian society; second, to cleanse society by eliminating real or imagined enemies. Throughout these campaigns, violence was widespread. It completely destroyed the trust and normal relationships among people. Instead of improving people's lives, these political campaigns disrupted regular production and farming activities and devastated the Chinese economy.

Consequently, Chinese people lived in misery. Hunger started to spread in the spring of 1959. Many villagers were reduced to eating tree bark or soil; thousands died of hunger. Children were sold by their parents in return for a dim hope of survival. Senior leaders in Beijing knew of the Famine as early as 1958. Despite the warning signals, Chairman Mao went ahead to launch his new campaign—the Great Leap Forward, an economic and social campaign aimed at transforming China through industrialization and collectivization. Mao showed very little regard to ordinary Chinese people's lives. For example, he famously said, "To distribute resources evenly will only ruin the Great Leap Forward," and, "When there is not enough to eat, people starve to death. It is better

to let half the people die so that others can eat their fill."[9] His Great Leap
Forward campaign turned an already bad situation into the worst possible
situation.[10]

As a student living in Beijing, the capital of China, my father was
initially shielded from the Famine that was widespread in the countryside.
Like the majority of Chinese people, he had extremely limited access to
information. There were no TV sets on campus. All newspapers and radio
stations were owned by the government. They only reported whatever
good news the government propaganda department instructed them to.
There was minimal substance in the news reporting because everything
was reduced to slogans and lies. For example, grain and steel production
figures were manipulated to always show progress—always going up,
never going down.

In the fall of 1959, based on a government directive, 200 students from
the Beijing Industrial School, including my father, were transferred to the
Beijing Chemical School. They were told that the government's needs had
changed, so they needed to switch majors. My father didn't know how the
government made such decisions. He didn't think much about it. He was
more concerned about having to learn new subjects.

Soon, his peaceful student life was interrupted. My grandfather came
to visit him. My grandfather initially told my father that he was on his
way to visit some relatives in the northeast of China. My father found it
odd that my grandfather would leave the village in the middle of the
harvesting season.   After my father's persistent questioning, my
grandfather finally told the truth.

The fall of 1958 had seen a fairly good harvest in my grandfather's
village.   However, since able male laborers were occupied at the
construction sites, children, women, and elders were left to handle the
harvest. Because they couldn't cope, much of the harvest was left to rot in
the fields. Similar things took place almost everywhere else in China. In
the meantime, higher-up party leaders insisted that communes must

---

[9] Yang, 2012

[10] If you want to know more about a broader account of the Chinese famine, I highly
recommend reading Yang Jishen's book *Tombstone*. As a journalist, Yang was able to
access many still secretive party archives so he was able to document what really took place
in China from 1958 to 1962.

produce more grain for cities in China and for other communist countries. Local leaders were either pressured into falsely reporting or just willingly exaggerated ever-higher grain production figures to their political superiors. The state then forced villages to sell more grain than they could spare, based on these false production figures. Even the seeds for the next year were used to meet government procurement. Very little grain was left at the village level. After the Chinese New Year in 1959, the village communal cafeterias ran out of food and had to close their doors for good.

Initially, the Shandong Provincial leadership transferred sugar beet residues from the northeast China into food to feed its people. But before long, they ran out of sugar beets, too. Villagers were left to fight for their survival unaided. Many villagers chose to flee to the northeast China because it was a well-known grain production site. Since many villagers were too poor to afford train tickets, some tried to sneak onto the trains at the station. Local communist officials were less concerned about the starving farmers than they were worried that these runaway farmers would make them look bad in front of their supervisors. They desperately tried to prevent the truth about the Famine from reaching the ears of the higher ups. Therefore, they set barriers outside the villages and near train stations to stop starving farmers from running away. To avoid being caught, desperate villagers tried to jump on the moving trains in the countryside and ended up being injured or, worse, killed.

My grandfather's first runaway attempted was unsuccessful, and he was caught by local officials at the train station. They locked him up for several days and sent him home with a threat that they wouldn't show any leniency next time. My grandfather knew that if he stayed, everyone at home would just starve to death together. He waited for a couple of days and tried again. This time, he was able to make it onto a train to Beijing.

Grandfather knew that my father was a student with no means to help him; he just wanted to see him before he headed to northern China. He didn't know what to expect in northeast China. Nor did he have any idea if he would survive there. But he was determined to find a way to keep his family alive, even if that meant he had to travel to a strange place with nothing but hope and determination. When my father saw Grandfather off at the Beijing train station, he didn't know if he would see him again.

Thankfully my grandfather safely arrived at Shenyang, the largest city in northeast China. Through his fellow villagers' help, my grandfather found a job as an apprentice for a factory that made bricks. His monthly salary was twenty yuan—less than three U.S. dollars. He sent most of his salary home so my grandmother could keep our family in the village alive.

Shortly after my grandfather's visit, my father's maternal grandfather—my great-grandpa Xiao—also visited him. Great-Grandpa Xiao was a self-taught medicine man. He used to work in a rural clinic. He told my father that Great-Grandma Xiao had died of hunger. In addition, the rural clinic had been shut down because so many people were dying of hunger anyway that no one cared to seek a doctor. After losing both his wife and his job, Grandpa Xiao had decided to migrate to Shenyang and find his son-in-law—my grandfather.

Great-Grandpa Xiao didn't come to see my father by himself. He brought my father's younger brother, Uncle Yulun, with him. Uncle Yulun was about twelve but looked more like a six year old; his head was too big in proportion to the rest of his body due to prolonged starvation. Uncle Yulun brought my father more heartbreaking news from home. My father's mother (my grandmother) had given birth to a baby boy in the spring of 1959. But she was too malnourished to have any milk to feed the baby and there was no baby formula available. As a result, she helplessly watched the baby starve to death in her arms. Had this baby survived, he would be my second uncle.

My grandmother was devastated. She didn't want to lose Yulun to starvation too. When she heard Great-Grandpa Xiao was going to Shenyang, she asked him to take Yulun with him. However, Great-Grandpa Xiao didn't want the fuss of a young child. So he came to Beijing, dropped Yulun off with my father, and then left for Shengyang by himself. He seemed unbothered by the fact that my father was a student who had no means of taking care of his young brother.

My father didn't have time to grieve for his family losses. His more urgent task was how to feed his little brother. It was almost impossible to find extra food, because students at Beijing Chemical School could purchase food at the school cafeteria only with school-issued meal tickets. How much each student could have for each meal was strictly allocated. As a result of this food ration, my father and his classmates were underfed. At that time, my father was sharing a dorm room with seven other guys. Every day, each one of them saved a bit of food from his allocation to feed Yulun. At night, Yulun and my father shared his tiny bunk bed. This arrangement lasted for two weeks, until my father found a way to send Yulun to Shenyang to reunite with my grandfather.

After sending Yulun away, my father realized that the living conditions back in the village were much worse than he had thought. He had to rescue his mother and his two young sisters. He had to find a way to get them to Shenyang to be with his father. He also realized that in order to make that happen, he needed to make some money as soon as the winter break started.

Most Beijingers didn't have refrigerators or freezers. Traditionally, Beijingers, from emperors down to ordinary residents, would hire someone to chisel ice from frozen lakes in the city. Then they would wrap up the ice in bags and bury them in underground cellars or storage areas. When summer came, they would use the ice to keep the house cool and the drinks cold.

Breaking ice from lakes was hard work with very low pay. Therefore, not many city people were willing to do it. The ice shop was delighted to hire peasant boys like my father, who were willing to work hard and get paid next to nothing. My father worked eight-hour shifts for just 90 cents a day. After 12 days' hard labor, he had earned 10 yuan and 80 cents, which was enough to cover his travel expense to go home. He got a train ticket as soon as he could.

Years later, he described to me what he saw back home. "When I walked into the village where I grew up, I could hardly recognize it. It should be dinnertime, but I didn't smell any cooking or see smoke anywhere. It was deadly silent. I couldn't hear any children cry or even dogs' barking. It was as if the time just stopped moving and something evil took all the lives away. I ran into my home. When I saw my mother and sisters, I couldn't hold my tears back. They were so thin and had barely any energy left to move. There was no food in the house except a few pieces of dried sweet potatoes, which already had mold on them. These dried sweet potatoes were special treats from the local government because of the Chinese New Year. I couldn't imagine what they had to eat prior to the Chinese New Year."

My father knew the first order of business was to get some food. He also knew that the only people who had food were the village leaders. Under the Chinese planning economy, nobody could buy any food without food stamps. There were two types of food stamps in circulation:

One was issued by the central government and could circulate nationwide; another one was issued by provincial governments and could circulate only locally. Only people who were living in cities were issued both types of food stamps. People who were living in the countryside were issued only provincial food stamps. Food stamps had values equivalent to money, but, of course, nobody dared trade them openly. National food stamps were much more valuable, because they could be exchanged for better food, such as refined flour. As a college student living in Beijing, my father had some national food stamps that local village leaders had no access to. Therefore, the local village leaders eagerly offered him some flour in exchange of his national food stamps. My father didn't mind the trade, because he knew that this was the only way he could get some food to sustain everyone at home for a couple of days.

Even though my father stayed at home for only three days, he got a chance to visit some other relatives. One of his cousins from the Li village invited him to attend a wedding. For the wedding celebration, his cousin's family roasted a pig, so the wedding guests had a good feast. My father was dumfounded by all the food that was served at the wedding banquet. His cousin's village was not too far from my father's. Why was one village full of hungry people while the other one had so much food? Among the wedding guests were Li village's Party secretary and team captain. They proudly revealed their secret to my father. Like the other villages, their males in the village had been forced to build irrigation systems the previous year. During the autumn harvest season, the Party secretary and team captain realized that if they didn't send their men home to harvest the crops, the whole village would face starvation in winter. However, they knew not to argue with their higher ups. Instead, they claimed that a couple of male villagers were sick and had to be sent home. In truth, these male villagers were sent back to harvest crops. When winter came, other villages had so many people starving to death that they couldn't even find people to dig graves, but at Li village, nobody was starving.

The village secretary and captain were poor peasants and not well educated. They didn't know many words except their own names, but they saved their villagers' lives with their street smarts and conscience. They told my father many tragic stories of people starving to death in other villages. My father was made to promise not to tell anyone else about Li village for fear that higher-up communist leaders would punish the village leaders.

These anecdotes only strengthened my father's belief that he had to get his mother and sisters out of there.

At dawn on New Year's Day, 1960, my father, with his three- year-old younger sister in his arms and a small bundle of clothes, walked out of the house he had grown up in, possibly for the last time. My grandmother held hands with her other daughter, walking right behind him. They didn't bother to lock the door because they didn't want to give other villagers the impression that they had run away. Except for the walls and the roof, their house was so empty that if a robber stopped by, he would be disappointed.

Their only hope was to leave this living hell as fast as they could, while not attracting any attention or getting caught along the way. Thankfully, they didn't encounter any problems on their way to the train station.

Figure 5. My grandmother, my father and his two sisters at the Beijing Train Station in the winter of 1960.

They first boarded a train to Beijing. After arriving in Beijing, my father bought them train tickets to Shenyang. Only after he purchased the tickets did he realize that he didn't have any money left.

My grandmother used a pair scissors to cut open a sewed inner pocket of her black cotton blouse and took out six silver dollars. She told my father that these silver dollars had been a wedding gift from her uncle, Mr. Zhou De Run. My grandmother had been hoping to give them to my father's future wife as a wedding gift, but now she had to part ways with them to save lives.

Each silver dollar had a smooth surface and carried warmth from my grandmother. My father had no idea how much these six silver dollar were worth, so he took them to the People's Bank of China. The staff paid him only one yuan (about 20 cents) for each silver dollar. If he still had those silver dollar coins today, each one would be worth hundreds of dollars. However, the six yuan (less than two U.S. dollars) saved his family's lives.

Three days later, my grandmother and her two daughters boarded the train to Shenyang to reunite with my grandfather. My father didn't know if or when he would see them again, so he asked the photo studio at the Beijing Railway Station to take a picture of him with his family.

My father was able to save his immediate family. However, he lost many family members and acquaintances during the Famine, including his baby brother, two uncles, his aunt and her family of five, his maternal grandmother, and Teacher Sun from his junior high school. The rest of China fared no better. Statistics show that the national mortality rate was 10.8 per 1,000 in 1957 and peaked at 25.4 per 1,000 people in 1960, the worst of the Famine years. Some regions suffered more than others. For example, the mortality rates in 1960 in Sichuan province and Guizhou province were at 54 and 52.3 per 1,000 people, respectively. Only Anhui province ranked higher, at 68.6 per 1,000 people.[11]

The Famine turned the entire country of China into a hell on earth. In his interview with the *Guardian*, Chinese author Yang Jishen mentioned that "People died in the family, and they didn't bury the person because they could still collect their food rations; they kept the bodies in bed and covered them up and the corpses were eaten by mice. People ate corpses

---

[11] Yang D., 1998

and fought for the bodies."[12] Unbearable hunger reduced people to animals. As Sir Basil Liddell Hart, the foremost military historian and theorist of his age, wrote in 1939: "Nothing undermines morale more decisively than hunger."

I cannot help wondering if the Communist Party members knew how horrific the situation in China was. They must have known, since they had eyes and ears everywhere. Yet their actions during the Famine were appalling. For example, China's grain exports to other socialist counties actually increased to four million tons during the years of the Famine.[13] The totalitarian regime showed it was more concerned about supporting its international socialist brothers and sisters than saving the lives of Chinese people. Deng Xiao Ping, the one who was credited for China's economic reform in 1980s, recommended in 1958 that if everybody could save a few eggs, a pound of meat, and a pound of oil, China wouldn't have any problem meeting its food export obligations to other socialist counties. Mao went a step further by suggesting a resolution that nobody should eat meat, even though his favorite food was a fatty meat dish.[14] These kinds of comments demonstrated how far removed the communist leaders were from reality.

In China, official archives about the Famine are still largely sealed by the government and difficult to access. We can only estimate that the death toll of the Chinese Famine ranges between thirty and sixty million.[15] To understand the scale of this atrocity, it is important to know that the estimated death toll for the World War II was sixty million. So Mao inflicted human suffering in one country equivalent to that of the entirety of World War II.

Many countries offered humanitarian aid to help China during the Famine, but the Chinese communist leaders refused. They would rather let people starve to death than lose face in the international community. There was also a strong belief that casualties were necessary for the sake of progress. Even today, schoolchildren in China have no idea about this

---

[12] Branigan, 2013
[13] Dikotter, 2010
[14] Dikotter, 2010
[15] Dikotter, 2010

darkest chapter in Chinese history, because history books published in China refer to the period from 1958–1961 as the "Three Years of Natural Disasters" or the "Three Years of Difficulties."

There was nothing natural about it. The Famine was a man-made atrocity by a totalitarian regime.

My father's childhood hardships—and especially the Famine—left a profound impression on him. I never see him waste food even today. In 2013, my parents visited me in Denver for a couple of weeks. I have an electric rice cooker. Every time the rice finished cooking, my father would scoop out the rice and pour water on the bottom of the rice cooker to soak it. After a few minutes, he would scrape the bottom of the rice cooker to get the rice that was stuck to the bottom so he could eat it. I said to him: "Dad, you are in the America now. We have plenty of food here. You don't have to do that." He answered, "In the old days, this much rice could save someone's life. Even today, someone worked very hard to grow this rice. You worked very hard to put it on the table. I respect all of your hard work, so I cannot waste it."

After my father went back to China, I started repeating what he did when I cooked rice. It has become a family tradition.

Food for Thought

If you google "China's Famine," you will see a lot of gruesome images. Yet in China, the Great Famine remains a taboo subject. Some people in China claim that Mao had good intentions. They believe that Mao merely misstepped in his implementation. The government hid official records of the Famine from the majority of Chinese people in order to preserve Mao's "savior of China" image. In fact, Mao's giant portrait is still hanging on the front gate of the Forbidden City Palace in the center of the Tiananmen Square.

The famed economist Adam Smith pointed out that intentions are not equivalent to results. Mao's Great Leap Forward movement was a classic example of government policies that fail miserably despite good intentions.

C. S. Lewis wrote in his essay "God in the Dock" that "Of all tyrannies, a tyranny sincerely exercised for the good of its victims may be the most oppressive . . . those who torment us for our own good will torment us without end for they do so with the approval of their own conscience. They may be more likely to go to Heaven yet at the same time likelier to make a Hell of earth."

Therefore, when we come across a self-proclaimed virtuous leader who has all the good intentions in the world, we ought to be vigilant and examine carefully the possible outcomes and unintended consequences of his proposals.

Is it any wonder that the road to hell is paved by good intentions?

CHAPTER 4

Fisherman's Daughter

While the land reform was tearing up villages and putting my father's family and millions of Chinese farmers through desperation and suffering, people who lived in the cities were subjected to different but equally brutal political campaigns. My mother was a city girl; her story will illustrate the differences.

My mom was born and raised in the city of Wuhan, the capital of Hubei province, in central China. With a population of 10 million, Wuhan is one of the largest cities in China. The city of Wuhan is made up of three towns: Wuchang stands on the right bank of the Yangtze River, while Hanyang and Hankou stand on the left side of the Yangtze and are separated by the Han River.

Founded as a capital city by one of the warlords during the Three Kingdoms Period (221BC–256AD), Wuhan's strategic location enabled it to play an important part in Chinese history. Wuhan was also one of the first port cities forced to open to foreign occupation after the First Opium War in 1841. On October 10, 1911, a revolutionary group led a revolt against the last emperor of the Qing Dynasty. This event, commonly referred to as the Wuchang Uprising, became the catalyst that kick started the Xinhai Revolution and led to the founding of the Republic of China. The Nationalist Party in Taiwan still celebrates October 10th as a holiday.

Besides rivers and revolutions, Wuhan is known for Wuchang fish, a freshwater fish that can only be found in LiangZi Lake. Wuchang fish is known for being tender, fat, and aromatic. It was one of Chairman Mao's favorite dishes. He even wrote a poem about it: "No sooner had I drunk water from the Yangtze than I savored Wuchang fish."

Of course, Mao didn't have to catch Wuchang fish himself, but my maternal grandfather did. Prior to 1949, my maternal grandfather, Zhou Shuanchen, a fisherman, made a living by supplying the local market with all kinds of fish. It was a tough life. He had to get up at four or five o'clock in the morning to go fishing and then take his freshest catch to the local market. Chinese people are picky when it comes to food. They are only willing to pay for the freshest catch. Whatever he didn't sell that day became food for his family. The profit margin in the fishing business was so low he couldn't afford a house. He and his family lived on a fishing boat, which was a cramped place. But he was content because he owned his boat and his family could stay under one roof.

My mother told me that she and her three siblings were all born on a fishing boat. Because my maternal grandma wasn't an able homemaker, my mother had to grow up very quickly. She learned to sew clothes and cook for her siblings at a young age. Wuchang fish was her favorite dish too, but she rarely had it. Grandfather sold any Wuchang fish he could catch because people were willing to pay more for this local delicacy.

My mother is truly a fisherman's daughter. The way she can consume a whole fish is legendary. When she eats fish, she wastes nothing. She will eat the fish meat, fish head, fish eyeballs, and anything else except bones. By the time she is done, all there is left on the plate is a complete set of fish bones.

Close to the end of the Chinese Civil War in 1949, the Communist People's Liberation Army procured fishing boats from fishermen like my grandfather so the army could ride along the Yangtze River to reach Nanjing, the capital city of the Nationalist Party. My grandfather was eager to help because he was tired of decades of war, violence, and uncertainty. He craved a peaceful life. Like most people in China, he didn't know what communism stood for, but he figured that he would give his support if the communists delivered the peace and prosperity they promised. He didn't realize that would be the last time he saw his boat.

After the communists liberated China, they initially showed tolerance toward private businesses, whether small vendors like my grandfather or large industrial enterprises. The government realized that after decades of war and destruction, the new regime needed experienced professionals such as teachers, doctors, engineers, and businessmen to rebuild the economy. But deep down, the communists were always suspicious of professionals and businessmen. They were too bourgeois for the government's taste. Ideologically, the communists believed that disproportionate private ownership was the main source of social injustice. Karl Marx, founder of communism, famously said, "The theory of Communism may be summed up in one sentence: Abolish all private property."

Gradually, the government, through nationalizing key industries such as banking and mining, controlled loans and raw materials that private enterprises badly needed. Besides taxing private enterprises heavily, new labor laws such as wage regulations drove up the cost of doing business. Soon, many private businesses were driven into bankruptcy. Government stepped in to lend a hand, which was really expropriation of private businesses' property. Many private businesses owners saw the writing on the wall and, one by one, "voluntarily donated" their businesses to the government.

In addition, the Chinese Communist Party targeted capitalists and business owners through the Three-Anti (1951) and Five-Anti campaigns (1952) in cities. The official goal of both campaigns was to root out corruption, embezzlement, waste and tax evasion. In truth, they became an effective tool to purge business people's opposition to the new Communist government.

As Frank Dikotter said, "Ideological purity went hand in hand with economic decline." My mother's home town, Wuhan, once was called the Chicago of the East. There had been a lot of hustle and bustle at the river port by the Yangtze for a hundred years. Now, hundreds of businesses closed their doors. Private markets shut down. My grandfather never got his boat back. He had no choice but to become a janitor at the city water facility. His income didn't improve and, more importantly, he lost his independence. He never touched his fishing net again.

In 1953, the Chinese government officially implemented a very strict household registration system called Hukou that was tied to the nationwide quota system for food and basic consumer goods rationing. Government determined the quantity of food that each person could have each month. On average, everyone received about 30 pounds of rice per month. Males would get slightly more than females.

Instead of using his own labor to earn food for his family, my grandfather and his family had to depend on government food rationing to survive. Distribution of food and other basics was strictly controlled by state-owned grocery stores. People had to present their household registration cards along with food stamps at government-run grocery stores before they could purchase food. The household registration system became an effective tool for the government to control the movement of people and distribution of essentials. People who attempted to move to different cities or even a different section within in the same city without government approval couldn't register under the household registration system, which meant they wouldn't receive their food ration. No government in 2000 years of Chinese history had ever restricted the Chinese people's freedom of movement like the communist government did. The Communist Party accomplished it merely four years after they were in power.

The household registration system also kept a close tap of people by documenting everyone's family background, occupation, and "individual status." Here are some samples of "individual status" categories recorded by the household registration system:

- **Good classes**: Communist party members, People's Liberation Army (PLA) soldiers, industrial workers
- **Middle classes**: Middle peasants, petit bourgeoisie
- **Bad classes**: Industrialists, business owners, intellectuals, professionals, anyone who studied abroad or had relatives abroad

In total, there were more than 60 class designations. My grandfather was designated an "industrial worker" because he now worked for the city government. However, since he had been a self-supporting fisherman (a small business owner) before the liberation, he was considered by the communists someone with a checkered past. Therefore, he and many others like him were forced to attend evening schools to be re-educated. My grandmother was forced to attend a separate evening school, which was run by a female communist. The fact that she was a housewife only made my grandfather look more bourgeois. A female communist said that it was demeaning that my grandmother spent her life serving her husband and children. She needed to work because Chairman Mao said that women could "support half the sky like men do" — which meant women could do anything men could do so women should man up. Since the communists wanted to liberate women from their traditional roles, women were encouraged to dress like men and hide their femininity. My grandmother ditched her flowery clothes and started to wear plain baggy clothes in either black or blue. As a matter of fact, every man, woman and child wore one of the three colors throughout China: black, blue, or gray. Only the military wore green. To dress plainly in limited colors meant no one would stand out.

Having conformity in outfits was not enough control for the communists. They also wanted thought reform. My grandparents were asked to transform themselves into new people by learning new slogans and right ideas taught by communists at evening schools. Everyone in their class also had to write self-criticizing essays, confessing all their personal faults and past mistakes. Sometimes they were asked to tell the faults of other students. Communists loved to turn people against each other because the less people trusted one another, the more they would trust the government.

This thought reform was truly a brainwashing process. It really should be called "thought control." Not only did people have no freedom of speech, they also had no freedom of thought.

Instead of the peaceful life that he dreamed of, my grandfather lived under constant fear that his checkered past might jeopardize his family's livelihood.

I never got the chance to ask him if he regretted lending his fishing boat to assist the communist liberation.

My mother's childhood dream was to become an artist. She liked drawing, but her family couldn't afford any drawing lessons for her. My grandfather learned through his re-education that artists were considered a borderline bad social class. Therefore, he encouraged my mother to learn some useful skills that the new society would need.

One of the direct consequences of re-education was self-censorship. It worked amazingly well and to the authority's satisfaction. When one's basic livelihood was totally dependent on the government, the result was absolute conformity. My mom dared not to mention her artist dream any more. After she graduated from her junior high, she enrolled in a nursing school because the school not only waived tuition, it also covered students' room and board. To help the students to learn about the human body, each dorm was given a full skeleton. Years later, my mother told me that she was so scared initially that she was afraid to get up at night during the first semester. I had to admit that the image of a full skeleton in a room probably was what made me decide not to pursue a medical career.

Figure 6. My mother (first to the right in the front row) with her nursing school classmates

Although the government proclaimed equality among men and women in many of their slogans, its policies sometimes were contradictory to their slogans. Based on China's food rationing system, as a female student, my mother received food stamps that she could use to purchase up to 30 pounds of food, while a male student could get up to 35 pounds of food.

The traditional diet in Wuhan had been fish and rice. But during the Great Chinese Famine from 1959-1962, there wasn't enough food for everyone. The government used sweet potatoes as a substitute for rice. Households were asked to bring their own containers to the fields where government workers distributed sweet potatoes. The sweet potatoes came with leaves and mud, which increased their weight. Prior to the liberation in 1949, sweet potatoes were considered peasants' food that city dwellers wouldn't touch. Sweet potato leaves were used to feed pigs, so even peasants wouldn't eat them. But when peasants in the countryside were eating tree bark and cotton seeds for survival, city dwellers could only be thankful that at least the government was providing them with sweet potato leaves.

According to Frank Dikotter's book *Mao's Great Famine*, the International aid organization considered 1,700 to 1,900 calories per day, which equals to about 51-57 pounds of unhusked grain per month, to be the minimum for a person's subsistence. Based on this standard, my mother's food ration was way below subsistence level. As a result, when she graduated from the nursing school in 1964 at age eighteen, she weighed only 90 pounds, even though she was 5'2".

My mother's graduation was a bittersweet moment. She didn't have any input as to where she would live or for whom she would work. No one bothered to solicit her opinion. Instead, she was told by her school administrator that she had to move to a small city called Zigong in Sichuan province, a place almost a thousand miles from Wuhan. Her employer would be a small clinic. Not all graduates shared the same fate as my mother. Some of her classmates were able to stay in Wuhan because they were either Communist Party members or members from a good social class with good connections.

She was afraid to say no to her school administrator. Worrying about losing food rations forced many young people like my mother to accept any form of employment anywhere the government assigned them. The school administration had already transferred my mother's *Hukou* (Chinese House Hold Registration card) to the clinic in Zigong. If she refused to go, she would lose her quota for food and other basic living essentials in Zigong, while the city of Wuhan wouldn't give her anything either since she was no longer considered a resident. Her family wouldn't be able to support her since they lived at subsistence level themselves. In addition, if she were to stay at Wuhan without proper paperwork, she would definitely be expelled from the city or even go to jail.

My mother said goodbye to her parents and her young siblings and took her first train ride from Wuhan to Zigong. She was only 18. She didn't know that a great change was about to happen to her family. She was too young to comprehend what was happening around her. She was sad to leave her family behind, but, in her young heart, she was also excited and anxious to find out what her new life would be. It took her an all-day train ride to arrive in the city of Zigong.

Zigong is located in Sichuan Basin, which is in northwest China. It was a midsized town with fewer than two million people. For centuries, it

Figure 7. The front entrance to Zigong Salt History Museum

was known as the "Salt Capital" for its ancient salt extraction technology and salt worship culture. Its most famous building was the Zigong Salt History Museum, originally built by salt merchants as a meeting place.

Since the salt trade historically enjoyed a government-protected monopoly, the salt merchants were well-connected wealthy people. Their meeting place has a splendid exterior and an exquisite internal structure and decoration, including many delicate stone and wooden carvings. Two stone carved lions stood in front of the main gate. Of course, after the communists took over China in 1949, the salt trade was nationalized and salt merchants were exterminated during various communist political movements. Their former meeting place was turned into a museum that focused on educating people about how the evil salt merchants exploited poor salt miners. When I was in school, we often had school trips to this museum.

After my mother arrived at Zigong, she realized that she had to make some adjustments. For example, people in Zigong spoke a different dialect than people in Wuhan, so it took her quite a while to understand what they were saying. More importantly, the local dishes were very spicy because the climate was humid. Local people believed that spicy food was good for their health. My mother not only got used to the spicy food quickly, she also learned to make some dishes using red chili peppers and peppercorns, like the locals did.

The clinic that my mother worked for was a small one. It had only two doctors and four nurses. Most of its patients were construction workers, since a nearby construction company was the largest employer in town. When my mother received her first paycheck, she discovered that the food stamps she received were enough for only 27 pound worth of food per month. This rationing amount was about three pounds less than she had received on a monthly basis in Wuhan. She thought that the Human Resource department had made a mistake. She had been hungry with 30 pounds of monthly food rationing. How was she going to survive on only 27? She went to talk to the staff at the Human Resource Department. One woman told her point blankly that only female *students* received 30 pound food ration monthly. Since my mother was no longer a student (they assumed she had stopped growing), she should eat less. No one seemed to notice that my mother was only 18.

Figure 8. My mother when she was nineteen (her hair was naturally curly).

Despite this reduced allocation, my mother had to send some food stamps back home to help her young siblings. I can't imagine how she managed it.

Even though my mother's official job title was *nurse*, she had to learn to do everything because there was a shortage of doctors in the clinic. Once a month, she had to work a full week of night shifts. The little clinic was busy because violence was very common. Initially, communist cadres beat up people who were designated as black class — intellectuals, business owners, landlords, capitalism sympathizers, and any other counter-revolutionary people. Later on, the communists broke into different divisions and fought one another. Some fought with guns, but most fought with rudimentary tools such as sticks and bricks. There were always casualties after fights, so the clinic became very busy. At least the clinic remained a sanctuary — because even the communists realized that they might need to see doctors sooner or later. My mother never expected she would be so busy, but she was fearless. Since she was a quick learner, in just a couple of years, her skills, medical knowledge, and experiences surpassed those of the two doctors.

My mother is a strong believer in fairness. She treated every patient the same way. It didn't matter whether the patient was a communist, an ordinary factory worker, or a member of a despised social class. She gave them the best care she could provide. Once there was a pregnant single woman who'd contracted a sexually transmitted disease. She had an uncle who lived in Taiwan, which was occupied by the nationalists, so she was assigned to a bad social class. In addition, she had relationships with several men, so the rumor was that no one knew for sure who the father was. This was scandalous in a small town. People despised her and called her a "broken shoe" — a Chinese slang term for a loose woman — to her face. By the time she was ready to deliver the baby, no other doctor or nurse wanted to touch her, because they thought she was dirty and unworthy. My mother was the only one who went to assist her delivery. When my mother realized that the baby wasn't crying, she wiped off the baby's mouth with a disinfected towel and performed CPR on the baby! Even the young mother was shocked. She wanted to kneel down on the floor to thank my mother for saving her and her baby's lives. My mother stopped her from getting out of the bed. She told the young mother to get a good rest because her baby needed her. My mother told me later that all she could think of at that time was to save the baby. She didn't stop for a second to think about any danger to herself. "Every human life is precious," she told me.

Under normal circumstances, the leadership of the clinic would want to recruit someone like my mother to join the Communist Party. However, she was criticized for lack of class hatred toward people belonging to the unworthy social classes.

Gradually, because my mother's technical skillsets were so solid, she became indispensable to the clinic. However, she never got a promotion or

Figure 9. Peony Flowers, painted by my mother

raise, since she was not a Communist Party member. Even after she won the first place in citywide medical knowledge test, all she received was a certificate. As a matter of fact, she didn't see either a promotion or a salary increase for seventeen years, until after she left Zigong.

When she retired in 2007, my mother picked up a paintbrush and started painting. In 2013, I organized an exhibition of her art works in Denver, Colorado. People loved her paintings so much that they bought almost all of her paintings.

My mother finally realized her childhood dream of being an artist, even though she had to wait for six decades.

Food for Thought

My grandfather loaned his fishing boat to the Communist Party because the communists promised a utopian society where everyone would have an equal share of everything. He was not alone. Many Chinese business owners made similar contributions to the Communist Party in support of liberation. Yet in return, the Party treated private businessmen as enemies of the new China — their property was confiscated for redistribution and they became targets for thought reform.

Gradually my grandfather lost his independence and became a janitor. But the government wasn't satisfied with controlling every aspect of his livelihood: what to wear, how much to eat, and what to do for living; it demanded full control of his mind too through thought reform.

Growing up in this environment, my mother tried to maintain her independent thinking by refusing to exercise class hatred and insisting on treating everyone the same way. The Party punished her act of disobedience by not giving her a raise or promotion for seventeen years, because a totalitarian regime doesn't need people to think independently, only to obey. Since part of being human is the ability to think and act independently, what the totalitarian regime did to the Chinese people was equivalent to stripping their humanity from them.

When I read George Orwell's *1984*, it gave me nightmares. It was exactly like what my mother and millions of other Chinese people lived through.

Thought control is as dangerous as a vampire who never dies. It still exists today in different forms. For example, in today's America, political correctness is another form of thought control. Many of us choose not to say what we want to for fear of being politically incorrect. Our self-imposed censorship shuts us up. But people in a free society should have the freedom to express themselves. That is why the first US constitutional amendment explicitly protects each American's freedom of expression, but political correctness violates that amendment. My grandfather's experience showed that losing liberty is a gradual process and it usually starts with limiting the freedom of expressions. The only way we can live freely is to speak the truth.

CHAPTER 5

The Sent Down Girl

My maternal grandparents had four children: three daughters and one son. Aunt San was the third child and the prettiest girl among her sisters. Unfortunately, she was born twenty years too soon. She was only fifteen in 1966, when Chairman Mao launched his most brutal political campaign: the Great Proletarian Cultural Revolution. Millions of Chinese people's lives were turned upside down, and this movement, unlike any other of Mao's political campaigns, hit young people like Aunt San especially hard.

If Mao ever had any good intentions prior to the Cultural Revolution (a big "if"), he probably had none left by 1966. His dozens of campaigns prior to 1966 systematically killed millions of people and destroyed millions of families. But as Joseph Stalin said, "A single death is a tragedy; a million deaths is a statistic." To dictators such as Stalin and Mao, ordinary people's lives were dispensable as long as they served their dictator's personal ambitions. Therefore, whether it was one person or a million people, Mao had no problem with using terror and violence to get rid of whoever stood in his way. Since Mao believed that his political power was weakened by the disastrous results of the Great Leap Forward movement, he started the Cultural Revolution as a cover to purge his personal and political enemies and grab power again.

Of course, Mao would never disclose his true intention to the public, so the stated goal of the Cultural Revolution was to remove traditional culture and Western culture from China and enforce Maoist doctrine. The part of the Cultural Revolution campaign that impacted young people the most was Mao's attitude towards knowledge. Mao advocated the idea that

"Knowledge is evil. The more knowledge one has, the more he becomes a counter-revolutionary." Paradoxically, Mao prided himself on being an avid historian. He liked to receive guests in his bedroom and show off the hundreds of books that occupied half of his bed. Maybe he just wanted to be only educated person in China and therefore fed the population an idea that even he didn't believe in. On the other hand, the doctrine makes perfect sense: An authoritarian regime always is terrified by well-educated citizens who think on their own. It is much better for the rulers if they can dumb down their populations.

Mao encouraged students to denounce their teachers and go on strike. Many high schools were closed and the university entrance exam was suspended, so the education system practically ceased to function. Since energetic young people didn't have to go to school anymore, they became a lawless but deadly force. They started destroying cultural relics and historical sites, but their attacks on culture quickly evolved into attacks on people. No one dared challenge them, since they branded themselves Mao's foot soldiers.

After these young people helped Mao get rid of his political enemies, Mao decided to restore stability in the cities by directing their energy elsewhere. Thus, Mao issued a new order: "Young people should go to the countryside and learn from the poor peasants." This decree gave birth to a new movement that came to be known as "Up to the mountains and down to the village."

A recent biography on Mao by Jung Chang shows what a hypocrite Mao was. Mao hated farming himself. As a matter of fact, he hated to do any kind of manual labor. Once again, he told people to do something he didn't believe in.

From 1966 to 1968, nearly all high school students and young adults were forced out of cities. Some were sent to the country; many were sent to the most remote and most under-developed areas of China. Over seventeen million young people were impacted.[16] My mother's three siblings—Aunt San, Aunt Er, and Uncle Tan—were forced to relocate to the countryside of Hubei province.

Aunt San was only fifteen when she and her siblings were sent to the countryside, but they weren't allowed to stay in the same village. The

[16] Wu, 2006

communists wanted to sever family ties so people could devote themselves 100% to the Party's causes.

Transition from a city girl to a peasant wasn't an easy process. Chinese farm work was very primitive. Mao believed that he had millions of people at his disposal, so why invest in machinery? Therefore, everything was done by hand. Aunt San's young and soft hands had never lifted anything heavy or touched anything filthy. Now, she had to toil in the fields like the other peasants.

For Aunt San, this meant that any field work that a peasant did, she had to learn to do also. Every day, Aunt San marched to the fields with other young people, following the lead of the local farmers and singing cheerful revolutionary songs along the way. In the fields, she had to plough, sow, rake, and weed. With a pole across her shoulders with a basket at each end, she carried human waste fertilizer.

Karl Marx famously said, "From each according to his ability, to each according to his need." But to the local Chinese communists, having needs was not sufficient to get food rations. Especially during the extended period of food shortage, local communists believed that whoever failed to show up in the fields should not eat. To them, it didn't matter if one worked hard or not, as long as he showed up. So Aunt San had to continue doing back-breaking labor even during her menstrual period. If she failed to show up, she would lose that day's work points. Without work points, she would not receive a food ration and would go on being hungry. It turned out that a food ration wasn't enough even for a girl, so she suffered famine edema. She wasn't alone. Some other girls couldn't stand the hunger, so they traded their bodies to village leaders in exchange for extra food.

Aunt San couldn't rest much in the evenings either, because daily evening study meetings were held in the village. The routine was to first bow to Mao's enlarged portrait on the wall and wish him to live forever. Then the groups would study books supposedly written by Mao (no other books were available). The most dreadful section of the meetings was when everyone confessed his bad thoughts or bad deeds. Sometimes these self-confessions turned into accusations of other people's bad thoughts and bad deeds. This daily exercise ensured no one trusted anyone else with his or her most intimate thoughts.

A year after Aunt San came to the countryside, she caught an infection in her left eye. The clinic in the village had only one staff member. Because he only knew how to deal with basic cuts, Aunt San asked the team captain if she could return to Wuhan to get treatment. The team captain accused her of being a spoiled "Miss Bourgeois Aristocrat." If she left, the captain threatened, her action would be equivalent to defying Chairman Mao's decree. The consequence would be very severe. Aunt San had witnessed one village woman being forced to parade around the village naked, with nothing but two well-worn shoes tied around her neck. Her crime was that her husband was a landlord. Aunt San knew that the captain wouldn't hesitate to use her as an example to intimidate other students. It was a well-known Chinese Communist Party's scare tactic to "Kill a chicken in order to scare the monkey." All these threats and accusations were too much for a sixteen-year-old girl, so Aunt San stayed in the village and continued to work. Due to lack of medical treatment, she lost the sight in that eye.

When I first met Aunt San, it was in the mid-1980s, and I was about eight years old. My mother and I first took a train ride from the City of Zigong to the City of Chong Qing. From the port of Chong Qing, we took a boat traveling along the Yangtze River to Wuhan and then we took several hours' bus ride from Wuhan to the village. Aunt San met us at the bus stop. She was nothing like I had imaged. Because she had been able to see with only one eye for so many years, her facial muscles seemed twisted and I was scared to look at her. Her skin was dark and rough. Years of hard labor made her look like my mother's aunt rather than her younger sister. She carried a shoulder pole with two bamboo baskets attached. She put me in one basket, our luggage in the other one. Then she bent her knees so my mother could help her to put the pole across her shoulders. When Aunt San started walking, the basket I was in swung gently back and forth. The rhythm quickly put me to sleep, so I don't know how long it took us from the bus stop to Aunt San's home.

My mother told me that Aunt San's childhood dream was to be a performing artist. If the Cultural Revolution hadn't taken place, Aunt San could have been a dancer or learned to play piano with her tender fingers. Harsh life in the village turned this delicate city girl into an ordinary farmer. Her beautiful looks were marred by the eye infection, so she didn't marry very well. Her husband, who'd only married her because he needed a woman, despised her looks, abused her constantly, and eventually left her for another woman. She raised her two sons and daughter by herself by working almost non-stop. During the day, she sweated in the fields like a peasant. At night, she cooked, fed the pig, cleaned house, and sewed clothes for her entire family. When I first met her, she was a typical peasant, and I could never tell that she had begun life as a city girl.

After Mao's passing in 1976, the youth who had been forced to the countryside started returning to the city. At the beginning, some returned to their home cities either on their own or in small groups. However, the cities that used to be their hometowns rejected them. They lacked the proper household registration paperwork, so they couldn't get food rations. Their families lived on limited food and could not support an additional mouth. Some returned youth were forced to go back to the countryside and some became homeless. However, as the years went by, more and more youth returned to their home cities in large numbers and became headaches for their local governments.

In the 1980s, the Chinese government gradually loosened its grip on the people. Minor reforms took place in both the countryside and in the city. In some regions, villages allowed farmers to sell some of their produce at self-organized markets and set their own prices. Street vendors, small shops, and private restaurants started appearing in the cities. These new businesses represented what the Chinese government called "individual economy," and they grew like weeds. Ronald Coase, in his latest book, *How China Became Capitalist*, mentioned that "the number of self-employed household businesses and single proprietorships increased from 140,000 in 1978 to 2.6 million in 1981."

The emerging individual economy gave hope to many people. A large number of them returned to their hometowns despite a lack of household registration paperwork. Aunt San and her siblings, along with their families, joined thousands of people in returning to Wuhan. The government initially didn't know what to do with them, so it pretended that they didn't exist. These people didn't qualify for government housing, so at the outskirt of the city, they built simple bungalows with whatever materials they could get their hands on. Gradually, they formed their own community. Many city people considered this neighborhood a slum.

A terrible fire broke out in 1992. More than half of the houses in the slum burned down to ashes.

Since Aunt San never finished high school, she initially had a hard time finding a job. She helped Aunt Er sell vegetables for a while. She also helped her uncle pull a rickshaw. Later, she took a job as a city sanitization worker, which was one of dirtiest, lowest paying jobs available.

When her ex-husband came back to her as a penniless, sick man, Aunt San took him in despite everyone's objections. She took care of him until he passed away, years later.

Aunt San's only son, Zhiwen, has only an elementary school education. He later became the first millionaire in our clan by running a successful publishing company. He begged Aunt San to quit her job and move out of the slum so she could enjoy his new mansion. Aunt San refused to move. She continued to live in the slum and to work as a sanitization worker. She was never embarrassed by what she did for living. She always told me that there is no reason to be ashamed of what you do as long as you are making an honest living. She continued to work until two months before her death, and only then because she was too sick to get out of bed. She didn't want to stay in the hospital, and she rejected any expensive treatment because she thought it was a waste of money. Her only wish was to be buried next to her ex-husband. She passed away in 2012, just after she turned 60.

Even though Aunt San passed away at a relatively young age, she was considered by many people to be a lucky person: She made it back to her hometown. She reunited with her family. She had a place to live. Her son became a millionaire. On the other hand, many young girls of Aunt San's generation who went to either the countryside or to the northwest wildness were raped, starved, or even murdered. Many of them never saw their families again, and many never made it even to age 60. Their families never found out where they were buried.

If these girls lived in a free society, they could be teachers, doctors, dancers, or any professionals they wanted to be. A dictator's decree altered their lives forever. They were China's lost generation. Today's Chinese history books gloss over this period as if these women never existed.

Food for Thought

Asian American director Joan Chen made a movie about the "Up to the mountains and down to the village" movement, which is called *Xiu Xiu: The Sent Down Girl*. It is about a 15-year-old girl from the city of Chen Du, Sichuan province, who was sent to Tibet to "study horses." But when this assignment was over, she was not allowed to return to Chen Du. She put herself in harm's way out of desperation, which led to a tragic ending. Seeing this movie made me think of Aunt San and many others like her. I highly recommend that you watch this movie and learn more about what young Chinese girls went through in that era.

Ironically, Chinese communists liked to brag that one of their greatest political achievements was to liberate women in China. After the take-over in 1949, the Communist Party established a special woman's department to organize and educate women, protect their interests, and help them become independent. Divorce and abortion became much easier. Every year on March 8, the International Women's Day, every work unit throughout the country recognizes their female workers.

It turned out that slogans, propaganda, and a national holiday didn't improve women's lives.

Why did Aunt San and many young girls suffer so much in the Cultural Revolution? These girls were sent away to the countryside at an age when they should be in school. A totalitarian regime who believes "ignorance is strength" always tries to dumb down its population while a free society welcomes educated citizen who can think independently. The truth is that women do not need special treatment or a special holiday. Both women and men are entitled to the same inalienable individual rights: life, liberty, and the pursuit of happiness. Women's lives only truly improve in a society that recognizes and protects individual rights of everyone.

Let's never forget that evil can come from the pursuit of progress. It happened in China. It could also happen anywhere else, including right here in the United States. Next time you hear a politician advocating another progressive policy, always remember to ask, "At what price?"

CHAPTER 6

When the Boy Met the Girl

While growing up, I was curious how my parents met, because my father is a country boy from the northern China, while my mother is a city girl from central China. When I marked their hometowns and Zingong, the city where I was born, on the map of China, the three locations were almost a thousand miles apart. When I brought up that question to my father, he said, "We have to thank Mao, because he was our matchmaker." Naturally, I thought he was joking. After some research about the broader historical background, I understood what he meant.

It was widely known that Mao had severe insomnia and could only fall asleep with the assistance of sleeping pills. I doubt that his illness had anything to do with millions of perished souls that he was responsible for. Probably, his constant fear of being attacked by real or imaginary foreign and domestic enemies kept him awake at night. [17] He warned his communist comrades that Western imperialists such as the U.S. and the U.K. were planning to go to war with China any time. Therefore, he wanted all of the Chinese people to be ready for war at a moment's notice.

The constant talk about the threat of war was a good strategy for transferring people's attention away from their miserable lives. As part of Mao's war preparation, any industry that the government believed to have a strategic importance, such as energy, mining, and chemical plants, was

---

[17] In her renowned book, *Mao: The Unknown Story*, Jong Chung, documented Mao's insomnia and suspected causes in great details based on the temporarily unclassified Soviet achieves on Mao.

ordered to uproot and relocate to the western mountainous region of China, to provinces such as Sichuan.

My father's major in college was chemical engineering. It wasn't his choice; it was chosen for him by the school administrators. Once upon a time, he wanted to become a pilot. However, years of inadequate food and malnutrition ruined his eyesight. He became nearsighted and had to wear eyeglasses, which enhanced his natural good looks and made him look like a young professor. Since chemical engineering was considered to be a strategic industry, he was told that, upon graduation, his employer would be Sichuan Chemical Science Institute in Zigong, Sichuan province, about 1000 miles away from his hometown in Shandong province.

Like my mother and millions of other Chinese youth, my father didn't have any say in where lived or for whom he worked. Of course, there were always exceptions to the rule. His classmates who joined the Communist Party were all conveniently offered opportunities to stay in Beijing, the capital city of China. In those days, becoming a communist was like winning a lottery, because the Party always took care of its own and gave them preferential treatment.

Unlike many of his classmates, my father didn't shed any tears when he left Beijing. He had an adventurous spirit. He took to heart the famous Chinese saying, "Traveling a thousand miles is equivalent to reading a thousand books." He concluded from his past experience that it was better to be mobile than to stay in one place for too long. As a matter of fact, he was rather looking forward to his new life in Sichuan, a place he had learned a lot about from Chinese history.

Sichuan can trace its history back to 15 BC, during the famous Three Kingdom Period, when one of the warlords, Liu Bei, established his kingdom there (AC 221-263). During the Sino-Japanese War (1937-1945), the Kuomintang government, led by the Nationalist Party, moved its capital from the city of Nanjing, Jiangsu province, to the city of Chongqing, Sichuan province.

The nationalists naively believed that the mountains surrounding Sichuan province would be a natural fortress that would deter enemy invasion. Therefore, during the Chinese Civil War (1945-1949), the nationalist government tried to make Sichuan its stronghold on the mainland. In 1949, when they realized that they had lost the war, their leader, Chiang Kai-Shek, fled to Taiwan.

Sichuan is not only known for its historical significance, but also for its reputation as one of the major agricultural production bases of China. Nature blesses Sichuan with rich soil, a mild climate, and the Yangtze River for irrigation. Because its grain production and pork output ranked number one in China for many years, Sichuan is historically known as the "Province of Abundance."

Sichuan was the most populous province in China. Once, it claimed to have a population of over 100 million. However, the Great Chinese Famine caused by Mao's disastrous economic policies turned the Province of Abundance into the Province of Shortage. Even though Sichuan's grain production went down, the central government increased its procurement of grain. It did so for three purposes: to support cities like Beijing and Shanghai, to export grain to support other communist countries like Vietnam, and to exchange for weapons and machinery with the Soviet Union. Thus, famine in Sichuan was more severe than anywhere else in China. During the three years' Famine, some 9.4 million people perished in Sichuan.[18] People outside of Sichuan didn't know much about this because the local Communist Party leadership made sure to block the spread of the news and stop hungry people from getting out of Sichuan. My father had no idea that his life in the university and in the capital was a sheltered one.

My father arrived at Zigong in 1965 and reported for duty at the Science Institute. His monthly food ration was reduced from 35 pounds to only 30 pounds. Now he realized that people lived much more difficult lives outside the capital. Under the government's relentless requisition policy, people sacrificed enormously to provide the essentials of living to the people in the capital. He couldn't help feeling guilty about it, even though he hadn't had a full stomach for as long as he could remember.

Hungry or not, life had to go on. As a good-looking young man with a college degree, my father was considered by many locals to be a great catch. His colleagues tried to set him up with girls they knew, but he politely declined their offers. He was determined to find love on his own. Fortunately, Cupid didn't make him wait too long.

Every day on his way to work, my father would pass by a small clinic.

---

[18] Cao, 2005

He first noticed my mother when she was talking to a patient at the front of the gate. Unlike most women, who wore their hair short, my mother was a pretty girl with naturally curly hair who usually wore her hair in a long braid. My father told me later that it was my mother's long, black, and silky hair that had first caught his attention, and he was pleased later that both his daughters inherited their mother's hair. He also noticed that my mother didn't speak the local dialect, so he guessed that she must come from somewhere else, like he did. He wanted to protect this beautiful girl who had been forced to come to this remote land all by herself.

After seeing my mother, he couldn't get her out of his head. So the next day, he intentionally stopped by the clinic and tried to catch a glimpse of her. He didn't know her name but he was too embarrassed to go inside and ask. I guess that's the effect a pretty girl has on a young man. Instead, he pretended he was reading the posters on the wall and hoped that she would come out. She didn't come out this time. He came back the next day and the day after. He did the same thing for the next couple of days and his behavior generated suspicion in the people inside the clinic. My mother heard people talking about this strange young man. She was not shy, so she went outside to confront him. She asked him what was so interesting in the posters. My father admitted that he just wanted to meet her. That was how the country boy from northern China and a city girl from central China met in a small town in western China.

My parents quickly fell in love. In spite of the government's decades of effort to replace normal human relationships with relationships between people and the Party, people still sought love because love is a more formidable force than the Communist Party. As Mother Teresa said, "The hunger for love is much more difficult to remove than the hunger for bread."

The two lovebirds always tried to find some time and place to be alone. That turned out to be a challenge. Both of my parents had to work six days a week. Most evenings, their work units organized various political study sessions to study Maoist thoughts. Therefore, they didn't have much free time for themselves. Sunday was normally their only free time, but there was very little entertainment available. The only movie theater in town showed the same revolutionary themed movies over and over again.

It got worse later when Mao's wife, Jiang Qin, directed eight model Beijing Operas. These model operas combined traditional Beijing Opera instruments with modern ballet movements. Their plots and dialogue were simple because Jiang Qin wanted to make sure the largely uneducated masses in China understood them. They told stories from China's recent revolutionary victories against foreign and domestic enemies such as Japanese invaders and evil landlords. These operas glorified Mao and credited him as the savior of China. No one could escape listening to them. They were played on the radios, in the theaters, on the stages, and blasted from loudspeakers in all parts of the country. They became the only entertainment people could get.

Fortunately, Zigong City Zoo still existed in the midst of all this turmoil. My mother told me that she and my father spent most of their time in the zoo, watching a few skinny animals that barely survived.

A year later, my parents got married. Their wedding was a simple one. Before they were married, they lived in separate dorms. When they decided to get married, one of their married friends lent them half of their room for a honeymoon suite. It was only big enough to put a twin bed and two suitcases. Fortunately, neither of them had many belongings. My father still wore black cotton cloth shoes handmade by his mother. He helped my mother put her bedding right next to his on the small twin bed. They used one of their suitcases as a table and another as a nightstand. That's all there was for setting up their first home.

They didn't have a wedding banquet, either. Traditionally, a Chinese wedding was a big event, full of rituals and customs. Having a wedding banquet is sometimes far more important than the actual wedding. Also at the wedding banquet, there are ceremonies such as the bride paying respect to her parents and in-laws by serving tea to them. However, under the communist rule, most of the traditional rituals and customs were banned. My parents' new home had no kitchen, so they had their first meal after being married at the cafeteria. My mother didn't serve tea to anyone. Instead, she and my father had to bow to a portrait of Chairman Mao. They bought some hard candy and handed them out to their coworkers, friends, and neighbors. This act served as their wedding reception. People were poor, so my parents didn't receive any wedding gifts except books by Chairman Mao.

The only thing my parents indulged themselves was in getting a

wedding picture taken at the local photo studio. My mother cut her hair
after she got married. Since having a big open smile in public is an act of
immodesty in China, both of my parents kept their mouths closed. But
from their wedding picture, one can tell that they were a good match. He
was handsome and she was pretty. They were both transplants to this
small town from faraway places. Neither of them was interested in joining
the Communist Party. Both simply wanted to make an honest living based
on their knowledge and skills.

Figure 10. My parents' wedding photo

My father believed that, if not for the government's forceful
distribution policy of young people, he and my mother probably would
never have met. That was why he called Mao a matchmaker. My mother,
on the other hand, chose to believe in fate. When I was young, she told me
a Chinese fairytale about the matchmaking god. He is an old man with a
long white beard. He has a thick book, the Book of Marriage Records,
which records all the names of single men and women in the world. He
also has a bag full of red strings. When he decides one woman and one
man should be married, he ties one end of the red string to the woman and
other end to the man. Therefore, no matter how far apart these two young
people are, they are bound to get married. Of course we mere mortals
can't see or feel the red strings; only the god can. So my mother likes to

say that she and my father are meant for each other because they are tied by the red string from god. After she told me this fairy tale, I checked my ankle frequently to see if there was a red string. I couldn't imagine whom the god had planned for me, but I thanked both the matchmaking god and Mao for bringing my parents together. Otherwise, I wouldn't exist.

Ironically, my parents got married around the same time when Mao started his notorious Cultural Revolution. Because of the disastrous Great Leap Forward campaign and the Famine, Mao lost some of his influence in the Communist Party. He gave up his chairmanship of the Party and the "reformists" in the Communist Party "elected" Mr. Liu Shaoqi to be the new chairman. Liu still had some conscience left. He gave the official verdict on the cause of the Famine as "seven-tenths natural and three-tenths man-made." Mao, on the other hand, claimed he believed that the Famine was caused by natural disasters such as drought, even though numerous pieces of evidence showed that the drought was not severe enough to explain the scale of the Famine. Mao was therefore greatly offended by Liu's conclusion.

To appease Mao's giant ego, Mr. Liu led the effort to build a cult of Mao, elevating Mao to godlike status. Mao's portraits were hung everywhere in China. The only books published in China were Maoist Thoughts. My parents told me that, in their work units, the first act to start a work day was for everyone to get together, bow to Mao's portrait in the office, and shout "long live Chairman Mao"; the last act to end the work day was for everyone to bow again to Mao's portrait and wish for him to live forever. In addition, every conversation they had in public had to start with a Mao quote. For example, my mother told me when she went to the grocery store, the store clerk would say: "Chairman Mao said 'People of the world, unite and defeat the U.S. aggressors and all their running dogs!' What can I get for you?" My mother would answer: "Chairman Mao said 'never to forget class struggle.' Can you give me a bottle of soy sauce, please?" My parents told me these crazy-sounding practices took place all over China. Failure to recite a Mao quote or showing the slightest disrespect to Mao's portrait often meant labor camp or death.

The cult worship of Mao turned out to be a fatal mistake for Liu. He failed to realize that Mao's apparent stepping back was merely a temporary break in order to take two steps forward. Mao could only be number one, not number two.

With Mao's estranged wife, Jiang Qin, and the ambitious Defense Minister Lin Biao's support, Mao launched the Cultural Revolution movement in 1966. The Cultural Revolution was in fact a clever act by Mao to reimpose his authority on the Communist Party and therefore the country.

Mao needed a political tool to purge his enemies. The self-proclaimed "Red Guards," which was mainly composed of over-zealous teenagers, became the perfect choice. These young people worshiped him feverishly.

Figure 11. Red Guards on the cover of an elementary school text book from Guangxi in 1971 (Giulia, 2010)

They were ignorant, but they were a deadly force.

Mao elevated the Red Guards' social status by appearing at a massive Red Guards' rally on August 18, 1966 at Tiananmen Square. Mao appeared atop Tiananmen wearing an olive green military uniform, the outfit favored by Red Guards. He told the Red Guards that China's communist progress was stalled by a growing privileged class. Mao encouraged the Red Guards to denounce any counter-revolutionary authorities, including his communist colleagues, who embraced bourgeois values and lacked revolutionary spirit. His main selling point was that no-one was better than anyone else and that the privileged class needed to be put down so China could be a true egalitarian and classless society.

No one, probably not even Mao, foresaw the damage that the overzealous Red Guards would do to the country. China almost fell into anarchy. The rule of law was suspended and was replaced by any organization that claimed to represent the right side of the revolution. High schools and colleges closed; factories and many regular businesses and—even many governments—were shut down. Professors, writers, scientists, artists, and even government officials were publicly paraded, denounced, humiliated, and tortured in public. Suicides among the persecuted were very common, but even death couldn't bring peace.

Among those who died was a famous Huangmei Opera singer, Ms. Yan Fengying. She came from Hubei province, just like my mother. Ms. Yan grew up in extreme poverty and was sold to a folk song tour group at a very young age. After China's liberation in 1949, she played a fairy in a popular movie about a folk legend. Her beautiful looks and her heavenly voice made her an instant celebrity in China. Many Chinese people, including my mother, were devoted fans of Ms. Yan.

During the Cultural Revolution, the Red Guards accused Ms. Yan of spying for the West by using her "vacuum tube radio to send telegrams to foreign masters." It was an ignorant charge because one cannot use radio to send telegrams. Unfortunately, this was an era when the ignorant was also the powerful. They shaved her head into a Mongol haircut, which they called yin-yang head: half her head bald, half her head with hair. She was paraded in mass rallies, and people shouted at her, "A complete confession is the only road to survival. Anything less will lead to death." She couldn't stand such humiliation and committed suicide.

The Red Guards wouldn't even grant her peace after she died. Instead, they claimed that she swallowed her vacuum tube radio. They forced an autopsy to look inside her stomach to search for the radio. Of course, they didn't find anything. But such atrocities and ridicule were very common in China during the Cultural Revolution.

People became so afraid that their self-censorship reached new heights. My parents told me that they had to destroy all their non-Maoist books to avoid any possible implications. Just as George Orwell described in his book *1984*, people started to check their thoughts carefully in every waking moment, even when they were falling asleep. Everyone, including the communist was afraid to speak to even those close to them about what was on their minds. Seeking safety, everyone denounced others and was denounced by others.

Few people other than Mao understood the true purpose of the

Cultural Revolution. The lawless situation created by the Red Guards was initially embraced by many ordinary people.

The Red Guards traveled all over China to spread Maoist thoughts and Mao's latest instructions. They ate and slept wherever they wanted to; no one dared to ask them to pay for anything. Since nobody was being productive anymore, and many places were shut down — including the science institute where my father worked — my parents managed to have a mini honeymoon. They rode the train from Zigong to Chendu, the capital city of Sichuan. On the train, they encountered a group of rowdy Red Guards who were rude to everyone. My parents initially tried to avoid any direct contact with Red Guards because anything could happen with them. It just so happened that one of the Red Guards suddenly had a seizure. His comrades started to panic when neither Chairman Mao's slogans nor his little red book could stop the seizure. My mother stepped forward to apply care to him. In her eyes, she saw only a sick patient, not a Red Guard. She was able to quickly cure the sick Red Guard. He and his comrades were so grateful that not only did they make sure my parents rode the train for free, they also let my parents stay for free at the best hotel in Chengdu, which was normally reserved for Red Guards. Many historical sites in Chengdu had been vandalized and destroyed by the Red Guards, but my father was able to show my mother around some of the remaining sites.

The Red Guards followed Mao's decree to denounce knowledge as useless. They condemned all authorities except Mao, even going so far as to publicly denounce their own family members. Their distrust of one another led to many divisions, and they fought amongst themselves constantly. Each group claimed only it knew and understood the true meaning of Maoist thoughts and Mao's latest instructions. They didn't just fight with their fists; they fought with real weapons, and many of them died in these meaningless battles.

My mother's clinic received many injured teenagers as a result of these senseless fights. She gave them the best care she could — not because she supported their cause, but because she felt sympathy for their youth and ignorance. These young people, many of them teenagers, didn't realize that their youth had been robbed by their great leader. In return for their sacrifice, once their great leader regained power, he sent them to the countryside to "learn from poor peasants." Many didn't make it back to the cities alive, or until at least a decade later.

The Cultural Revolution brought ordinary people nothing but suffering. There was a shortage of everything: food, cooking oil, cloth, bicycles, and so on. Everything was rationed via stamps. For instance, every person, adult or child, received an allotment of three ounces of cooking oil each month. Meat was hard to come by. Families who were fortunate to get hold of some pork would use the pig lard to supplement cooking oil.

It was at this time that my mother was pregnant with my sister. My father was traveling for business in Shanghai, the largest and most developed city in China. He desperately looked for something nutritious that he could bring back to his wife and his unborn child. Someone told him that a local cafeteria was killing a pig for the upcoming Chinese New Year celebration. He knew that they wouldn't sell him any pork because private transactions like that were strictly forbidden. But he was a very persuasive man and he could be persistent. He was able to convince the cafeteria staff to give him some pig lard. In exchange, he offered his engineering skills to fix the oven for them.

By the time he got on the train back to Zigong, the small town in western China where his family lived, his most precious cargo was a small aluminum pot that contained pig lard. The train ride home was about 12 hours long, and the train was crowded with half-starving, hollow-looking people. He knew that a pot of pig lard would be enough to cause a riot. Nothing strips humanity away like hunger. Thankfully, my father always had a quick wit, so he told the people who surrounded him that the pot contained highly secret equipment for the Cultural Revolution. If anyone touched it and caused it to malfunction, he would be a counter-revolutionary. Being accused of being a counter-revolutionary was a serious crime in China. It meant labor camp, persecution, or even death. My father put Mao's little red book on top of the pot and then let the pot sit in the center of the folding table. For 12 hours on a crowded train that was full of hungry people, nobody touched the pot. That was how my father got the pig lard home to his pregnant wife and their unborn child.

Not everyone had the kind of resolve my father had. The limited food ration was especially hard on his coworker Big Li, so called because he was a big and tall guy. One Sunday morning, he went to the cafeteria to get steamed buns for breakfast for his wife and three children. He bought five buns. Initially, he ate his share, because he was too hungry to wait. Then he talked himself into eating another one, because he reasoned that his two younger kids could share one. One by one, he ate all five buns before he walked out of the cafeteria. When my father discovered Big Li, Big Li was sitting by the side of the road, crying. He told my father what had happened and that he was too ashamed to go home to face his hungry family. He told my father, "I am a selfish pig. No, I am worse than a pig." My father took two steam buns from his basket, put them in Big Li's hands, and said to him, "This is all I can spare. Go home and bring this to your family. Remember, you are a man." Big Li brought the two buns home, but he couldn't face his wife's disappointed gaze and his kids' hungry cries. He chose to end his despair by jumping into a lake.

People in the community avoided discussing Big Li's death, because people who committed suicide were believed to have crimes to hide.

Ordinary citizens like Big Li were not the only ones caught up in man-made tragedies. Events that were even more shocking took place in China. In October 1968, Chairman Liu Shaoqi was expelled from the Communist Party in spite of the numerous self- criticisms he did both publicly and privately. He became the Enemy Number One of the Communist Party. No one ever saw him in public again. He was thrown into a secret jail without trial even though he had held the office of the President of China. Shortly after, he died in jail after extensive torture and disease. He was cremated right away under a fake name. None of his family knew he died until years later. Of course, very few people in China learned about Liu's fate until the Cultural Revolution was over.

Liu, the President of China, and Big Li, an ordinary citizen, had one thing in common: the Chinese Communist Party neither recognized nor protected their right to life.

Food for Thought

Mao's Cultural Revolution movement was probably the darkest chapter in China's history. The name Cultural Revolution is very misleading. It should be called "Cultural Destruction," as it aimed to control every aspect of an individual's life: how much one could eat; what if any education one could get; whom one could work for; where one could live; what entertainment one could have; what thoughts one could have. By taking the decision-making ability from individuals, the regime denied the Chinese people their individual rights.

In his speech to a joint meeting of Congress on June 27, 1990, Nelson Mandela said, "To deny people their human rights is to challenge their very humanity." China's Cultural Revolution was Mao's war on humanity.

Was Mao the sole person responsible? What about the Red Guards? Those young people called themselves "Mao's red solders" with their fanatic worship of Mao that solidified his godlike status in China. They claimed that "knowledge is useless." And Mao wasted no time in taking advantage of their ignorance. As Martin Luther King, Jr. said: "Nothing in the world is more dangerous than sincere ignorance and conscientious stupidity." The Red Guards carried out the evil biddings of Mao like mad dogs, denouncing any authority except Mao. They were responsible for physically and psychologically attacking Mao's political enemies, intellectuals, their own teachers, and sometimes even their own parents. Those young people were responsible for many innocent deaths and the mass destruction of Chinese cultural heritage. I am always thankful that my parents had the wisdom to avoid this craziness. But it was clear that they were in the minority.

What did the Red Guards receive in return for their loyalty? Once Mao was done using them, he sent them to the countryside and wilderness for the next two decades. Many of them never made it back to cities to reunite with their families. Even of those who made it back, many couldn't obtain decent jobs because they hadn't received any education or learned any useful skills.

Young people in America today are facing a different set of challenges. Many of them have gone through watered-down education, received useless diplomas, and are walking around with no real skills and no job prospects but heavy loads of student loan debt. Despite this, they keep voting for the political figures who put them in that situation to begin with. I can't help wondering: Are our young people making the right choices today?

Fouad Ajami, a senior fellow at Stanford University's Hoover Institution, pointed out that "Dictatorship often rests on a measure of consent, as people acquiesce in their own servitude and forge their own chain." Mao's Cultural Revolution might be an extreme case in world history, but that doesn't mean it won't reemerge in various degrees, shapes, and forms in other countries. The lesson from the Cultural Revolution has universal implications.

Are you forging your own chain right now?

CHAPTER 7

Walking Tall

It was ironic that the Chinese Communist Party promised Chinese people an egalitarian society, yet the Communist Party wasted no time in establishing a class system in China as soon as it liberated China in 1949. All people in China were classified into one of more than 60 categories. There is no doubt the Communist Party's policy was shaped by Mao belief that: "In class society, everyone lives as a member of a particular class, and every kind of thinking, without exception, is stamped with the brand of a class."[19]

During the Cultural Revolution, the Red Guards simplified the class system to two basic categories: red vs. black or friends vs. foes. Initially there were five subcategories of black class: Landlords, rich peasants, counter-revolutionaries, bad elements/rightists. Quickly, capitalist roaders and reactionary academic authorizes were added, so there were seven subcategories of black class.

The Red Guards were fanatic about not only the red vs. black classes, but also lineage theory, which stated that if one's parents belonged to one of the red classes, one was born red, as a natural revolutionary successor and future master of the world. On the other hand, once someone was designated as a black element, his family members and descendants suffered. Children inherited the class labels of their fathers. The Red Guards believed that bad blood would pass on from one generation to the next, so children of the outcasts were subjected to constant humiliation and

---

[19] Mao, 1937

discrimination, sometimes even violence. There were many youths, eager to be accepted by society, who chose to publicly denounce their families. Some would spit on or beat their family members with the bottoms of their shoes.

The Red Guards' fanatic belief in lineage theory seemed odd to many people, because the concepts of kinship and family lineage are deeply ingrained in traditional Chinese culture, which is influenced by Confucianism. The Cultural Revolution typically denounced any traditional Chinese culture practice as feudalistic and bourgeois. I guess that it was a lot harder to remove Chinese traditional culture than the communists chose to believe.

My parents initially thought that since they grew up poor, they had nothing to hide and nothing to worry about. They didn't realize that a dark cloud was hanging over them. My father's trouble was traced back to something he did while he was in college. After he witnessed the living hell his family and other peasants went through during the Famine, he naively thought that the Famine was caused by a few bad apples in the local leadership level. Therefore, he wrote a letter to the central government to report what he saw: hundreds of people starving to death. The central government sent his letter back to the county leadership, who, in turn, passed a copy to the Communist Party secretary of the village. Rather than admitting any wrongdoing, the village communist party secretary sent a letter to the Communist Party leadership of the Beijing Industry University, where my father was a student. In his letter, the village leader claimed that my great-grandfather was a landlord and that he and his family had been angry with the result of the land reform. My father's letter about people starving to death was a lie with the goal of denying the People's Commune's progress. Therefore, they advocated punishing him.

Curiously, the Communist Party leadership of the Beijing Industry University never told my father about either letter. They never punished him. Instead, they put copies of both letters into my father's personnel file.

There is something you should know about the personnel files in China. Like the household registration system, a personnel file was another powerful tool for the government to apply total control over its people. Everything about a person was documented in detail in his personal file: what social class he was born into; where he went to school;

where he had been; the backgrounds of his parents, spouse, and children; what employment he held; what organizations he belonged to; what rewards and punishments he received; and even what his thoughts were.

One's personnel file behaved like one's shadow. It followed one everywhere and never went away.

My father had no clue what was in his personnel file. Only a privileged few could view it. After the Cultural Revolution started, the fact that Great-Grandfather was classified as a landlord was brought up again in the village. My father received a letter from his father, in which Grandpa informed my father that he was classified as landlord because of Great-Grandfather. My father thought that was unfair. He remembered growing up poor and had to fight hunger constantly. How could his

Figure 12. My father before the Cultural Revolution

family be classified as landlord? He also was deeply concerned about how this classification would impact his own children. At this time, my sister was three and my mother was pregnant with my brother. My father thought that if he didn't do anything, his children would grow up wearing invisible black letters on their foreheads. He wanted to protect his children from the humiliation, so he wrote a letter to the village Communist Party secretary and made a case that his family should be classified as poor peasant, not landlord.

The village Communist Party secretary sent a letter along with a copy of my father's letter to the Communist Party secretary of the Science Institute, accusing my father of being historically counter-revolutionary. Like every other institute, the Science Institute was given a quota from higher ups to uncover a certain number of black class people within the organization. The Party secretary of the Science Institute got hold of my father's personnel file and he was more than glad that he could use my father's case to meet his quota.

Soon after, my father was detained by the revolutionary guards from the Science Institute. In the lawless China, every organization had the power to arrest anyone. The rule of law was suspended indefinitely. There was no due process, no trial. Even if one was innocent, there was no guarantee of survival. The Party secretary announced my father's crime in public and put him into a labor camp for re-education. Anyone in China could be sent to re-education labor camp for four years or more without a trial. There was nothing educational about those labor camps. Detainees in camps were required to work for 12 hours or more per day with little food and no pay. Similar situations took place in many other parts of China. Millions of people were persecuted and sent to labor camps in order to fulfill or surpass the quota handed down from the government. Some historians estimate that there were on average 10 million Chinese people in various labor camps and prisons in any given year under Mao's rule.[20]

When my father was detained, my mother was giving birth to my brother in the clinic she worked for. Her coworkers hid the news of his detainment from her, but the Communist Party secretary of the Science Institute decided to inflict more pain on my father. He went to the clinic after my mother's labor and announced the "crimes" that my father committed. He tried to coerce my mother into divorcing my father. She refused. Before he left, the secretary threatened her, advising her to think about it again, because she and her kids would suffer if she remained married to a counter-revolutionary.

My mother was scared. She had heard horror stories about labor camps. Prisoners in the labor camps were made to do all kinds of tough and dangerous work, such as reclaiming wasteland and extracting minerals underground. They were poorly fed and sometimes prisoners resorted to cannibalism. From the moment my mother learned about my father's arrest, she couldn't produce any milk to feed my brother, who was just born and hungry. Her coworkers cooked very watered-down rice porridge to feed my brother. My poor brother never had a single drop of mother's milk. He suffers some health issues even today, which made my mother feel guilty. She believes that she was responsible for my brother's poor health because he didn't have any mother's milk.

---

[20] Chang, 2005

My mother wasn't allowed to visit my father at the labor camp until six months later. She took my sister and my brother with her for the first visit. When she saw my father, she could hardly recognize him. He had lost a lot of weight and he hadn't shaved for a long time. He called my sister's name, but she was so scared of her surroundings and my father's ghostly look that she tried to hid behind my mother. My father turned to my brother; it was his first time meeting his son. He wanted to hug my brother, but the guards stopped him. Their shouting caused my brother to cry. Soon, my sister started sobbing too. The guards, who didn't want to be bothered by crying children, ordered my mother to take her kids and get out of the camp.

Years later, my father told me that one of the cruel punishments he received inside the labor camp was to move big piles of bricks from one end of the courtyard to the other. After he was done, he was ordered to move them back again. At the end of the day, he felt his back was going to kill him. Yet he kept his chin up and walked tall. He never confessed any crime, and neither did he accuse anyone else. Now, when I read about the Greek myth of Sisyphus, a king who was eternally condemned to roll an immense boulder up a hill, only to watch it roll back down, I have the image of my father moving bricks from one end to the other end of the courtyard.

My father spent three years in the labor camp. He was only allowed to have family visit once every six months. His salary was suspended. My mother, sister, and brother lived on my mother's salary alone, which was about five dollars per month. But my mother always made sure my sister and brother put on their best clothes to visit my father. She knew my father didn't have enough to eat inside the labor camp. Guards often took the food ration meant for the inmates for their own consumption. My mother always tried to save whatever food she could get and bring it to my father. During each visit, my mother put on a brave face. She never cried in front of my father or the guards. My sister tried to cheer everyone up by singing some revolutionary songs she had learned from the kindergarten. Those were the only times that my father couldn't help his tears from streaming down his cheeks.

My mother never gave up fighting for my father's release. Since my mother was the best doctor in the clinic and had helped many people in the community, people, no matter which side they were on, they never gave her a hard time. They all realized that no matter how the revolution went, they would need a good doctor sooner or later. My mother's persistence finally paid off, and my father was released in 1973. He was very fortunate. Many people didn't survive the labor camps — the Chinese gulags — at all.

After his release, our family life got back to normal. A couple years later, I became the newest addition to the family. I was always considered a lucky baby because I was born right before the Chinese government rolled out its One Child policy. That policy was one of the most controversial and most hated forms of intrusion into people's lives. If my mother had waited another year to get pregnant, I wouldn't exist — because forced abortion is common in China, in order to enforce the One Child policy.

When my mother was pregnant with me, my father thought he would get another son. He picked a boy's name for me, which was Qiang. Once I was born, my mother asked him if he should give me a more girly name. He told her that Qiang had many good meanings: excellence, strong, tough, exceed. He wanted me to live a better life than he did, and he wanted me to achieve more. So I was born a girl with a boy's name.

Since my father wasn't able to spend much time with my brother when he was a baby, he tried to make it up to my mother by taking extra care with me. I developed a deep bond with my father from a young age. From the time I could walk, I would stand by the door and wait for him to come home after work. Whenever I saw him, I would run towards him. He would pick me up and plant a big kiss on my cheek.

My father has always loved literature. However, at this particular time, there was very little literature available to read, other than government sanctioned literature on class struggles and translated books from the Soviet. Even books for children were full of propaganda. He bought me some pocket-sized comic books about communist war heroes and read them to me. I had an amazing memory from a very young age. Each time, after he read a book to me, the next day, I would read the same stories page after page to my playmates. The adults around me thought I had learned how to read already. They didn't know that I had only memorized what my father'd read to me.

When I was old enough to go to kindergarten, my father's bicycle became our main transportation. Every morning, he put me in the front basket; my sister sat at the back, and my brother sat in the middle. My father pushed the bicycle first to elementary school to drop off my sister and brother, and then to the kindergarten to drop me off. My happiest moment at the end of the day was when my father showed up to pick me up from kindergarten. I couldn't wait to tell him what I learned that day. He always magically produced something to reward me. Sometimes it

Figure 13. My brother Jian, me, and my sister Min at a park (left to right)

was a button; sometimes it was a piece of hard candy.

However, life likes to make unexpected twists when one is least prepared. On a hot summer day, I was waiting for my father to pick me up at the kindergarten. He never showed up. Later, I found out that a truck made a sudden turn, crashed into his bike, and ran over his right leg. He suffered a great deal of blood loss, and there were so many pieces of fractured bones, the doctor told my mother that the only way to save him was to amputate his injured leg. My mother said no. She told the doctors that my father was only 37 and he had three young children. He couldn't lose his leg. There must be another way to save him. Later, my mother was able to find an old Chinese bone-setting doctor who was willing to give it a try. He prescribed a lot of herbal medicines and, once a week, would give my father acupuncture treatment.

We as a family were held together by the strong will of my mother. She gathered us around her and told us to keep our chin up because Daddy would walk tall again. My brother had poor health when he was young, so he was constantly on some kind of medication. My mother's monthly salary was mostly spent on medicine for my father and my brother. All of us basically lived off my father's salary. Since his accident, he received only 50% of his salary. The truck driver who'd injured him didn't pay any punitive damage, because there was no such concept in Chinese law.

I didn't remember if we ever bought any new clothes. My mother sewed everything for us: underwear, pants, shirts, skirts, and coats. She crocheted sweaters. We wore hand-me-down clothes. Often, my mother would turn something she wore into something for my sister. Once it became too small for my sister, my mother would adjust it again for me. We didn't have either a washing machine or a dryer. In fact, no one did. So my mother, later with the help of my sister, had to hand wash everything.

Under the communist regime, any kind of decoration, unless it was revolutionary themed, would be seen as bourgeois. All men had the same haircut. Most women cut their hair short as well. My mother's hair was naturally curly. So every morning, she put a hot towel on her hair for a few minutes to straighten it. No female wore lipstick, makeup, or any accessories. Everyone—men, women, and children—wore one of the three colors: blue, gray, or black cotton that faded after frequent washing. The more ragged the look was, the better. Most people dressed like that to blend in with the masses. They were afraid to stand out. But my mother always made sure to add some new elements, such as an embroidered small flower or animal on my hand-me-down clothes. She thought that no one would object to this kind of embellishment on a child and this was her way to be a little rebellious against the social norm. No matter how difficult life was, she always made sure that our clothes fit and were comfortable and clean.

I don't know whether it was because of my parents' strong will or the power of herbal medicine or the magic of acupuncture or the combination of all of the above, but my father gradually got better. Eventually, he was well enough to learn to walk again, but it proved to be a long and painful process. I watched him go from using two crutches to one crutch, from moving from one side of the bed to the other side of bed and then to the door. His facial expression and his sweat told me that every step was agonizing, yet I never heard him complain or moan.

It took him two years to be able to walk tall on his own again.

During this long and excruciating recovery period, he not only learned how to walk again, he also taught himself English. After the new China was founded in 1949, and especially after the Korean War broke out, the communist government launched the Hate America campaign. English was treated as a manifestation of imperialist exploitation. No one was willing or allowed to learn English. The only foreign language one could learn was Russian. My father learned some Russian in college. During his recovery period from his injury, he initially tried to pick up Russian again from a Russian and Chinese dictionary.

However, the political climate gradually changed. After Joseph Stalin's death, Mao and the new Soviet leader, Nikita Krushchev, had different interpretation of Marxist ideology. Krushchev's denunciation of Stalin made Mao uneasy. Mao constantly worried someone like Krushchev existed in the Chinese Communist Party. With Mao's support, the Chinese Communist Party formally denounced Krushchev as a revisionist traitor.

The Soviets pulled their economic and military support of the Chinese Communist Party. The dispute between China and Russia opened the way for normalizing the relationship between China and the United States. Mao, for instance, invited the U.S. Ping-Pong team to visit China. Rumor said that he initiated the "Ping-Pong Diplomacy" because he wanted to choose a sport that he knew the Chinese could win. After President Nixon's visit to China in 1972, learning English became less taboo and there was a gradual new demand for people who knew English. However, years of isolation meant that there were few resources available to learn English.

My father started teaching himself English. His teacher was a dictionary: English to Chinese. He recited the dictionary word by word. Later, when the Chinese government gradually loosened its control on the Chinese people, my father started translating foreign engineering articles into Chinese. By the time he retired, he had become a renowned expert within the chemical engineering community.

Physically, my dad never fully recovered from his injury. Over the years, he had a dozen more surgeries to remove the remaining bone fragments from his leg. Despite this, throughout his life, he has been determined not to let that tragic accident cripple him physically or mentally.

Someone once said that "Life is like a game of cards. The hand that is dealt you represents determinism; the way you play it is free will." My father certainly has been dealt some very awful hands in life's card game. However, he played them with determination and a strong will. Eventually, he became a winner against all odds. Many years later, when I heard the song "Walk Tall" by Ziggy Marley, I felt that it was written for my father. It says "Walk tall . . . Stand tall. . . . Nothing is ever gonna keep me down. I jump over hurdles I'll come around."

My father is the most influential person in my life. I inherited his love for literature. I'd like to think that I inherited his good looks, too. More importantly, his struggles and triumphs have had a profound impact on me. I learned from him to always tell the truth, to always strive to learn new things, to be persistent and never give up.

My father is in his mid-seventies now. Most people at his age would stop learning new things and just relax. My father learned how to use a computer when he turned 70. He is fascinated by new technological development. He sends me emails of anything he reads that he believes I should know about.

He is also fascinated by America as a country. He has a big map of the United States on the desk in his study.

I used to travel a lot for business. Then and now, before I travel, I always call him to let him know which city I am traveling to. He looks it up on the map with the assistance of his magnifying glass and tells me which state the city resides in. He always asks me to bring a map of the city back. When I come back from my trip, I call him again and he quizzes me about the city I visited — about things such as population, climate, and important businesses. He never loses his curiosity.

Food for Thought

Many people suffered a fate similar to my father's but didn't survive. My father only survived because of his iron will and the strong family support that my mother provided. My family paid a dear price for its survival, but the hardship only brought us closer. The older I get, the more I look up to my parents as role models and appreciate them.

When the Party secretary asked my mother to divorce my father, he was deploying a common technique in the communist regime. He knew in order to break my father's mind, he first had to break my father's family. The communists long held the belief that, in order for the Communist Party to have absolute loyalty from its people, it had to first break down the close ties within families and communities. The Party forced friends to denounce one another and family members to betray one another during persecutions. Consequently, the traditional warm hospitality among Chinese people disappeared. Everyone became fearful of one another and stopped trusting and relying on one another. When people threw themselves at the feet of the Communist Party for mercy, the Party knew that it had the upper hand.

G.K. Chesterton said, "The family is the test of freedom; because the family is the only thing that the free man makes for himself and by himself." To examine if citizens of a particular country are free or not, all you have to look for is whether they have strong families. A free society is made up by strong families, while in a statist society, the state takes over the caregiver role.

It concerns me deeply that one of the most obvious unintended consequences of the welfare policies in the U.S. is the collapse of marriages and families. A single woman with a child receives more welfare benefits than if she gets married. How could a low-income young man Is it any wonder that back in 1963 (before LBJ initiated the Great Society program), only six percent of children in the U.S. were born out of wedlock; yet today, that number has increased to forty-one percent—and fifty-three percent for children born to women under thirty?[21] Along with the increase of single parenthood is the decline of fatherhood. According to the U.S. Department of Health and Human Services, fatherless children are at a dramatically greater risk of drug and alcohol abuse, mental illness, suicide, poor educational performance, teen pregnancy, and criminality. The Heritage Foundation's analysis also shows that children raised by

---

[21] Tavernise, 2012

single parents are twice as likely to be poor as adults.

No one can be truly free if he or she is chained to the welfare system, and children are paying the price for the choices that their parents make. Maybe it's time to focus on rebuilding stronger families in this country and relying less on the state.

CHAPTER 8

"We Recognize Nothing Private"

I was born at the tail end of the Cultural Revolution, which was officially over with Mao's death. My father told me years later that he could feel the gradual political changes after Mao's death in September 1976. Before, no one dared to challenge Mao's godlike status, his ridiculous economic policies, or his brutality against his opponents and the Chinese people. Shortly after Mao passed away, the senior leadership of People's Liberation Army (PLA) arrested the Gang of Four, who were Mao's four most loyal followers and included his wife. Mao's appointed political heir, Hua Guofeng, became the puppet leader of the country. However, the real power was held by the generals who'd fought alongside Mao through the revolution and survived Mao's purge during the Cultural Revolution. They understood the discontent of the Chinese people, but they also worried that admitting Mao's wrongdoings would weaken the communist rule in China. Thus, the Gang of Four conveniently became scapegoats for Mao and the Communist Party, and took all the blame for the Chinese people's three decades of misery. The Gang of Four was put on a show trial and, of course, was found guilty. The members received life sentences.

The Communist Party decided that Mao's public image as great leader and savior must be preserved. A memorial for Mao was built on the corner of Beijing's Tiananmen Square and Mao's body was mummified and has been on display ever since.

Eventually, Deng Xiaoping emerged as the new leader. Deng granted the Chinese people a bit more freedom. Ordinary people's lives were slightly better than in the past, but not by much. The damage that the Cultural Revolution had done to China was so severe that it would take decades to recover.

As far as I can remember, there were very few things in my life I could call mine or ours. Sharing was an integral part of growing up in China. By the time I was born, my family of five shared one bedroom within a row of low ceiling bungalows. My mother made a curtain to separate it into two rooms. My mother, my sister and I shared a large bed in the inner section. My father and my brother shared a smaller bed in the outer section. We didn't have a family kitchen. No one else had one either. Every family had a little cooking area with its own coal burning stove in a communal kitchen across from the bungalow. Because the ventilation of the communal kitchen was very poor, during dinner time, it could get so smoky that one could hardly see.

Figure 14. Our happy family. Picture was taken after the Cultural Revolution was over.

Everyone from the bungalow shared two public restrooms: one for men, one for women. The women's restroom had only a few squat-down toilets. People had to bring their own toilet paper when they had to go. A single light bulb hanging on the ceiling provided dim light. Once that bulb burned out, nobody bothered to change it because no one was responsible for it. Therefore, going to bathroom at night could be quite an adventure.

Another reason that no one cared to change the light bulb probably was we didn't have electricity all the time. Power shortages were very common. Usually each district took a "voluntary" turn to have its power shut off for one day per week in order to guarantee power usage of key industries. When there was no power, often there was no running water either. Therefore, we often stored water in any containers we could find. We carried this habit to the present day. I remember when my American husband Mike and I visited my parents in Wuhan in the summer of 2009, we were told that it was our district's turn to have no electricity for a day. My parents and I were filling up every container in the house with water, while Mike, who never experienced this before, was dumbfounded.

We didn't like to live without electricity, but there was something we would rather live without – public noise. No matter where we went, we shared the noise, because there was always a loudspeaker somewhere, either at the street corners or in the park or in public squares. It was impossible not to hear it. The loudspeakers started everyday around six a.m., so no one could sleep in. The speakers all played the same communist-themed music first, and then a high-pitched female voice from the only government-run radio station would read daily news. It always started with the activities of our "great" communist leaders. There was very little international news. During lunchtime and in the evenings, they played revolutionary songs, read more news, or sometimes broadcasted political speeches.

As the youngest child in the family, I learned from early on that being the baby had clear advantages and disadvantages. My sister is six years older than me. Since she witnessed my father's imprisonment, she matured quickly and became a good helper to my parents at a young age. Due to the persistent food shortage, my parents often had to get up at three or four o'clock in the morning to stand in lines in front of two different grocery stores for a pound of sugar or flour. My sister was left behind to take care of me. Chinese babies used diapers made out of used clothes. After each change of diaper, Chinese people didn't throw the diaper away; instead, they washed it and dried it under the sun so it could be reused. My sister often got the undesirable assignment of washing and changing diapers for me. For this, I am forever grateful.

My brother is the middle child. He is four years older than me. In most of my childhood memories, he took his big brother role way too seriously and never ceased to torment me whenever he could. Years later,

I learned from my husband (who has two younger sisters) that it was what a big brother was supposed to do to his younger sister — to toughen her up.

We used to raise hens when we were young, mainly for their eggs. The eggs were precious because they were the only nutrition we could get on our own. However, since there was not even enough for people to eat, we didn't have much to feed the hens. As a result, the hens didn't produce eggs every day. So only the youngest or the sickest person in the family got to have an egg. My brother didn't believe it was fair for me to enjoy this special treatment as the baby of the family. Once, he put me under the bamboo basket meant for the hens. He got a good spank from my parents. However, a typical boy, he seemed to have a short memory for spankings. It didn't take him long to come up with some new tricks to give me a hard time.

On the other hand, he also did something very nice for me. One day, he and I were home alone. He was seven and I was three. I told him I was hungry. He tried to cook fried rice for me. He didn't know how to light the coal stove, but he knew he was supposed to mix pig lard with rice because pig lard made everything taste delicious. Therefore, he added almost half a jar of pig lard into the raw rice. Fortunately, my mother came into the kitchen just in time to discover the mess he had made. He didn't get a spanking that time.

Since no one owned a TV, the main entertainment for our community was outdoor movie showings. The movies were free of charge. They took place in the public square only a couple times a year, so it was always a big deal. On movie night, every family brought stools and chairs to the square before dinnertime. After dinner, adults would gather at the square, chatting with one another, while we kids ran around. There was a lot of laughter, and it felt like a festival. Several younger kids, including me, had the best seats. On a concrete pedestal in the center of the square, stood a statue of Chairman Mao, waving one hand as if he were still leading us towards utopia. The pedestal was wide enough that several of us could sit by his feet. We had the center and front view that no one could beat. Since we were young, nobody fought us for our prime seats. Most of the movies we saw were either Chinese movies or movies from the Soviet Union such as *Lenin in October*. Almost all movies were revolutionary related and had predictable plots.

After China and Japan normalized their diplomatic relationship in the late 70s, imported Japanese movies became popular in China. I guess that people were hungry for something different. I remember watching a Japanese movie in the public showing and for the first time I saw a man and woman kissing on the screen. Everyone, especially the adults in the audience, became visibly uncomfortable. Public displays of affection between adults were not socially acceptable in China. My mother told me to cover my eyes, but I had to ask her, "What are those two people in the movie doing, Mama?" Before she could answer, my brother looked at me as if I were the biggest idiot in the entire universe and said, "They are making love!" My mother covered his mouth in a hurry, but I was sure that everyone heard him. How do boys always know these things?

Not all public gatherings were as fun as movie showings. Besides outdoor movies, the government liked to publicly denounce and execute criminals. We knew an execution was coming when we saw large posters around the public squares. The posters listed criminals' names and their crimes. A bloody red X always covered the entire page, which meant these people were condemned to die. My parents would never let us witness any public executions. I was told that those criminals' families were forced to pay for bullets that were used to shoot their loved ones. Later, when I grew a little older, these kinds of executions were moved to the countryside so people in the city didn't have to hear the gunshots. However, posters that announced crimes still showed up at public bulletin boards. The bloody red X haunts me.

My parents tried to shelter us from the external turmoil as much as they could. They never bought into the Red Guards' slogan that "Knowledge is useless." My parents are strong believers in education. They learned from their own experiences that education is the only way that an ordinary person can change his life. Thus, they tried to find all kinds of educational activities to keep us busy.

When my mother found out that one of our neighbors was a retired art teacher, she took the three of us to his house and asked him to teach us drawing. He was hesitant at the beginning, because art was still considered bourgeois. She promised him that she would be held responsible if something happened. We went to his house once a week and came home with assignments to draw circles, triangles, and squares again and again. I didn't know then that my mother's childhood dream was to be an artist. I just found this exercise incredibly boring.

Then my father asked an old gentleman in the neighborhood, Mr. Wei, to teach us Chinese calligraphy. We had to learn to write Chinese characters with brush and ink. To save money, we practiced on used newspaper. My parents were meticulous in inspecting the newspaper first, so they could carefully remove any pictures of communist leaders

Figure 15. My sister demonstrates Chinese Calligraphy. The gentleman standing next to her was her teacher Mr. Wei. He lived until he was 95.

before we wrote on it. My father told us a horrible story that happened to one of the neighborhood kids. He happened to sit on a newspaper with a big picture of Mao. People in the neighborhood accused him of being a counter-revolutionary. He was arrested and sent to the labor camp despite only being 11 years old. We had to be extremely careful.

It turned out my sister excelled in Chinese calligraphy. She won a national award for her calligraphy. My brother excelled in drawing. I wasn't very good in either subject. However, my parents wouldn't cut me any breaks. They knew I had an excellent memory, and they were determined to put it to good use.

After the end of Cultural Revolution in 1978, the political and cultural environments in China started to loosen up. The local newspaper began to publish an ancient Chinese poem once a week. Of course, the editor always made sure to add an editorial analysis right underneath the poem to educate readers on interpreting the poem on a class struggle basis. My father would cut only the poem from the newspaper and glue it to pages inside a Maoist book, since there were no other books available. He would explain to me what the poem meant based on his own understanding and made me recite them. Every Sunday, I would stand in front of him and not only recite the new poem I'd learned, but also poems I had learned in the past. I didn't like it at all. Only years later did I realize that memorizing these poems gave me a good literature foundation and is probably largely responsible for my good essay writings skills. More importantly, I still remember many poems today, even after living in America for more than a decade.

Both of my parents were good at math, so they started teaching me simple math before school officially started. When I turned five-and-a-half, my mother took me to the local elementary school. The school administrator told her that I was too young for the first grade, because most first graders were seven years old. My mother is a persistent and persuasive person. She believed that I was ready for school, so she convinced the school administrator to test me on math and reading. Since I passed both tests easily, the school administrator accepted me under the condition that if I didn't do well on the midterm, I would quit the school until I turned seven.

I didn't know the agreement between my mother and the school administrator; I was simply excited to be able to go to school like my brother and sister. On the first day of school, I asked my mother to comb my hair into two pigtails tied with two red ribbons. I carried the one shoulder school bag that my sister used when she was in the elementary school. It was originally made out of green canvas. This kind of bag was first widely used by military personnel. It became popular during the Cultural Revolution by the Red Guards. A fashionable outfit for the Red Guards would be the green People's Liberation Army uniform with a big belt and a one-shoulder green canvas bag. Later, almost all schoolchildren carried this kind of bag. When I got the school bag from my sister, it was so well worn and washed that it was hard to tell it had been originally green. I never liked the faded, used color. I wanted a new backpack like some of my friends had, made out of colorful plastic. But I knew better than to ask my parents for one.

Years later, when I learned young people in the West intentionally washed new jeans to fade them or cut holes in them, I couldn't help being puzzled. Why did they want their new clothes to look old and beaten down? I suppose that when one has so much stuff to choose from, to have something that seems old is one way to stand out.

When I was in the first grade, my classes consisted of six subjects: Chinese literature, math, politics, music, drawing and P.E. The school day started at eight in the morning. We normally had three classes in the morning, alternating between Chinese literature, politics, and math.

After the first two classes in the morning, it was time for forced morning exercise. Whether in school or in the workplace, everyone had to stop what they were doing and join the exercise. Every public space was equipped with a loudspeaker. The loudspeaker in our school courtyard would blast revolutionary music and a woman's high-pitched voice would say, "Our Chairman Mao wants us to be healthy so we can build the future of Communist China!"

There were two portions of exercise. The first part was the eye exercise. It consisted of a set of movements with our eyes and was supposed to prevent us from becoming nearsighted. Of course, it was always difficult for little kids to keep their eyes closed for even a minute. I often covered my eyes and peeked between my fingers, and I would normally find other kids also peeking through their fingers. I believe that schoolchildren in China are still forced to perform this eye exercise on a daily basis. There is little scientific proof that this exercise ever helped prevent nearsightedness.

The eye exercise lasted about 10 minutes. After that, everyone had to get out of the classroom to do 15 minutes of calisthenics. We gathered on the playground. The woman from the loudspeaker guided us to do all kinds of body movements such as stretching arms, kicking, and bending over. All couple hundred of us, including teachers, did the same movements. The routine lasted for the next 12 years, until I graduated from high school.

In the afternoon, we would have music, drawing, and P.E. class. In my drawing class, we learned to draw with pencils first, and then colored our drawings with crayons. My drawing teacher praised me for the circle and square that I drew. I didn't tell him that my parents had made me practice these shapes way before the school started.

In music class, we didn't learn any musical instruments because the school didn't have any except an ancient piano that badly needed tuning. As a result, our music teacher taught us to sing revolutionary songs. Group singing was popular in China because it was much safer than singing solo. No one had to stand out. Whether in schools or at the workplaces, there were always group singing performances or competitions during major holidays such as International Worker's Day or Independence Day. On each major holiday, every class in the school would take turns to stand on the stage to sing together and compete against other classes of the same grade. We had to wear uniforms: white shirts and blue pants. Adults had their own group singing competitions. My parents normally participated in group singings in their respective work units and they generally received a piece of soap as a "thank you for participating" from their work units.

I didn't enjoying singing that much, but in a group setting, no one cared. I did enjoying learning. By midterm, I scored 100% in math and 100% in Chinese literature, and became number one in the class even though I was the youngest. That was a first in the elementary school's history. Afterwards, nobody suggested quitting school to me anymore. As a reward, my parents bought me a new school bag, a bright orange backpack. Backpacks had just become popular in China, so not many kids had one. Neither my sister nor brother had one. They were jealous and I was on cloud nine.

My parents had high expectations for us. They made their expectations known, too. We were expected to do well in school. Failure was never an option. When I brought any test result home, my father always asked if I was first in the class and if I had scored 100%. If I wasn't either one of those, he would ask me if I had learned from my mistakes and would promise that I wouldn't repeat them.

A student's test score was never private information. After each exam, teachers would write everyone's name and score on the blackboard in the back of the classroom. When it was time for parents and teachers' meeting, every kid's name and his or her overall class ranking would be posted on the blackboard. Parents of the children who ranked in the top 10 would take the front row seats, while parents of the children who ranked in the bottom 10 would hide towards the back of the classroom. My parents never said it out loud, but I knew for sure that they expected to always sit in the front row.

While I was growing, big political changes were taking place in China. The arrest of the Gang of Four didn't stop the power struggle among the communist leadership. Mao's appointed heir, Hua Guofeng, pardoned one of Mao's generals, Deng Xiaoping, without realizing that he had just signed his own political career's death sentence. Deng carefully mobilized his supporters within the Party and ousted Hua from his top leadership position by 1980. Deng then became the most powerful man in China.

Of course, most Chinese people had no idea of the kind of power struggles that went on within Beijing's Party leadership. People could only read the tea leaves through subtle changes in life. For example, Deng's elevation to China's new number-one figure took place when I had just started elementary school. I remembered that at first, the first two pages of every textbook were pictures of four Communist Leaders: Karl Marx, Friedrich Engles, Mao, and his appointed successor Mr. Hua Guo Feng. When I was in second grade, Hua's picture disappeared.

Deng was a controversial political strong man. From the early revolution till the early years of Cultural Revolution, he did much of Mao's evil bidding. From the early 1950s to early 1960s, Deng was the Party chief who was in charge of Southwest Sichuan province. According to Frank Dikotter's book, *The Tragedies of Liberation*, Deng carried out systemic killings, the final death toll of which exceeded Mao's quota. Deng extracted excessive grain procurements in order to meet export needs during the Great Chinese Famine, turning the Province of Abundance into a living hell and causing millions of people to die of violence or hunger.

During the height of the Cultural Revolution, Deng fell out of favor with Mao. Mao, who trusted no one, was suspicious that Deng would seek to rewrite the history of the Cultural Revolution after Mao's death. The Gang of Four, with Mao's permission, began the Criticize Deng and Oppose the Rehabilitation of Right-Leaning Elements campaign. Thus Deng himself became one of the most notorious counter-revolutionaries in China. He was stripped of his official duty, and he and his family were sent to a labor camp per direct orders from Mao. His eldest son was pushed off stairs by the Red Guards and became paralyzed from the waist down.

Chinese people were forgiving. After witnessing Deng and his family suffering, people gradually forgot about the systematic killings he had headed when he was in charge of Sichuan in the 50s. There was something unique about Deng as a politician. Deng could be ruthless like any other communist strongman and crush his political enemies without mercy. On the other hand, he also was a strategic and pragmatic guy. He famously pronounced that "It doesn't matter if a cat is black or white; he's a good cat as long as he catches mice."

Deng's political pragmatism was reflected on many levels. He liked to maintain control from behind the scenes. He was smart enough not to plaster his own picture everywhere like Mao did. He never held office as the head of government or the head of the Chinese Communist Party. Instead, he was a firm believer in Mao's famous saying that "Power comes from gun barrels," so he had the Chinese military under his firm control. He was the supreme leader of China from 1978 to 1992, and nothing could get done without his approval

Deng recognized that if he openly denounced Mao like Nikita Khrushchev had Stalin, he would weaken the communist rule in China. Instead, he continued to publicly support Mao's status as a "great Marxist, proletarian revolutionary, militarist, and general," while being the first leader to point out Mao's legacy was "seventy percent good, thirty percent bad."

Deng's practicality showed on a diplomatic front. He became the first Chinese communist leader to visit the United States in 1979. He held negotiations with the United Kingdom over returning Hong Kong. The final agreement was reached based on his "one country, two systems" philosophy, which refers to the coexistence under one political authority of areas with different economic systems: communism and capitalism.

Deng is mostly credited for China's economic reform. However, the reality is more complicated than most people assume. The Chinese Communist Party leadership proved that they knew nothing about economic development in their first thirty years' rule. Therefore, in the early 1980s, many economic reforms were first introduced by local leaders, not directed by central government policies. If the reform was a success, it would be adopted by larger and larger areas and ultimately introduced nationally.

One of the famous examples is that of 1979, in Xiaogang village, Fengyang County, Anhui province, where 18 households signed a contract with their village leaders. The leaders secretly allowed farmers to be responsible for the profit and loss of their own households. Extra production exceeding the government quota belonged to the farmers who produced it. Farmers were allowed to sell their extra produce in the market. The village leaders ran the risk of being executed as counter-revolutionary if this arrangement was discovered. Farmers agreed to take care of the leaders' families if that happened. This gamble paid off. The arrangement proved an instant success and the standard of living of the local farmers increased in a very short time.

Deng demonstrated his pragmatism in his readiness to lend his support to an economic reform idea if it was tested successfully on a small scale. When Deng heard of this experiment, he personally praised the village leaders. The village leaders were not punished. Instead, their method was adopted by other regions throughout China, and it became the "household responsibility system." It was under Deng's leadership that the Chinese government loosened its grip on Chinese people on both the economic front and the political front.

Our living standard improved under Deng. By the time I was in third grade, our family had moved into a three-story apartment building. Each floor had about ten apartments. We shared a public restroom on our floor. Our apartment was the one right next to the public restroom, so the smell could be intolerable in summer. Yet we had two and half rooms, including our own little cooking area inside our apartment. We didn't need to cross the street to cook anymore. We felt like we were in heaven.

The new apartment was right next to my elementary school. My parents made sure we picked up some household chores. When it was my turn to cook rice, my mom tied our house key around my neck with a long red string. During the morning break between the second and third class, I ran back home to put rice in a cooking pot, add water, and then set it on the stove. By then, our stove was upgraded from coal to natural gas. I learned how to light up the gas stove and keep the fire at minimum. Unlike today's rice cooker, with its automatic shutoff, the mix of water, rice, and fire strength all had to be perfect so rice wouldn't get burned. My parents would never throw away any food. If the rice was burned, we ate it.

There was a big jar containing propane that stood next to the stove. When the propane was out, my parents had to ask someone from the station to deliver a new jar. Carrying a heavy tank of gas and climbing two flights of stairs was a backbreaking job. My parents warned us that if we didn't study hard, that was the type of job we would end up with.

Shortly after we moved to the new apartment, one of our neighbors bought a black-and-white TV. He became the star of the neighborhood.

We crammed into his living room to steal a look at this strange box that showed pictures of people who were talking and moving. There was only one channel — the Central China Television Station (CCTV). Most of the broadcasts were news and propagandas. In the evening, though, the TV showed domestic TV series or movies from other communist countries, such as Russia and Yugoslavia.

After Japan and China reestablished a diplomat relationship, CCTV also showed some Japanese TV series. The most popular one was about a group of young Japanese women training to play volleyball. Most of their movements were unrealistic. For example, one of them could jump in the midair, flip her body 360 degrees, and then smash the ball. But we didn't care. All the girls in the neighborhood were mesmerized by the show. It probably also helped that the male volleyball coach in the show was good looking. Nobody dared to point that out.

There were only a few volleyballs available in the school, so the high school kids got to play with them. We elementary school kids had to invent something of our own. We played with balls made out of newspaper and pretended we were those Japanese volleyball players with their fancy moves.

A lot of change came when I was in the third grade. In addition to moving to a new apartment, my father published his first translated article on chemical plants. He received an honorarium of 20 yuan ($2.5) from the publication. It was equivalent to half of his monthly salary. He'd never had any income source outside of regular wages, and he hadn't had a salary raise for more than a decade, so he was excited not only to see his name in a magazine, but also to receive some extra money. We made dumplings that night to celebrate his newfound success. This time, there was more meat than vegetable inside the dumplings. None of us realized then that more changes were coming our way.

Food for Thought

Vladimir Lenin, the founder of the Soviet Union, once explained the totalitarian worldview this way: "We recognize nothing private." Mao certainty implemented this view to its fullest extent.

Why do communists hate privacy? Because they want absolute control, and the only way to do that is to control people's intimate thoughts and behaviors.

The totalitarian government in China showed no regard for people's right to privacy, because there is no "individual" in communism. The regime accomplished the invasion of privacy by enforcing conformity in every aspect of people's lives: from communal living to omnipresent loudspeakers to mandatory mid-morning exercises to group singing competitions. Everything was designed to replace individual choices with the government sanctioned collective way of living and thinking. "Conscience was no longer a private matter but one of state administration."[22] Under the disguise of sharing everything, people buried their individual identities and became indistinguishable parts of groups. The crowd density gives the illusion of equality because "All who belong to the crowd get rid of their difference and feel equal."[23]

One way to fight back is to think independently. It takes tremendous courage to be an independent thinker. I am grateful that my parents are strong believers in the power of minds. They did everything they could under difficult circumstances to get us the best education possible from early on. Their no-nonsense approach and high expectations pushed me to be the best I could be.

Why is privacy important to a free man? As Peggy Noonan said, "Privacy is connected to a personhood." Having privacy is part of being human: We are entitled to keep our own intimate thoughts and deeds from outside world invasion. Without privacy protection, people will feel their personhoods being threatened, and they will censor their thoughts and expressions. Therefore, a person without privacy protection cannot live freely.

Today in America, our privacy is endangered by increasing government surveillance in the name of security. From TSA to NSA, history shows that the growing power of the state is always accompanied by the shrinking stature of individual rights. My fellow Americans, is that a price you're willing to pay?

---

[22] Arthur Miller
[23] Canetti, 1962

CHAPTER 9

Why Not Me — First Political Indoctrination

Among all the classes I took in school, I wasn't a big fan of physical education (P.E.) class. We didn't have a gym (not that I knew what a gym was until I came to America) or much equipment. We rarely did anything fun. Mostly what we did was track and field exercises — a lot of running: from 50 meters to 200 meters, later increased to 800 meters when I was in high school. We also did a lot of jumping, such as long jumping in the sand box. We also did a lot of sit-ups. Every year, each of us had to pass a national P.E. standard test based on age and sex, but regardless of body type or preference. For example, we were required to do at least twenty-five sit-ups in a minute in order to pass.

In P.E. classes throughout China, students were doing pretty much the same track and field exercises. Later on, when China returned to the Olympic Games, I was surprised that China couldn't get more medals in track and field competition, since that's all Chinese kids did in P.E. classes. Years later, when my American-born husband told me he did fun activities in his P.E. classes, such as playing dodge ball, I just wanted to punch him.

Besides track and field exercise, we did physical work. My class was divided into small teams. Every day after the classes were done, teams took turns sweeping the classroom floor, cleaning the blackboard, and emptying the trashcan. Whenever the school needed some external cleaning up, we would have no class for half a day. We would be outside, pulling weeds, picking up fallen tree branches, and doing whatever our teachers told us to do. Older kids had to clean bathrooms and plant or remove shrubbery. It was no wonder that our school never had to hire a janitor.

However, even pulling weeds was tolerable compared to the political pressure put on our young shoulders. The communists never wasted any time in indoctrinating youth into its political ideology. Children were compared to a sheet of blank paper. The Party wanted to make sure to put down communist ideas as soon as possible.

All schoolchildren were expected to join an organization called the Young Pioneers of China (YPC). It was a massive nationwide organization and had branches in every school in China. Everything about it from flag to organizational structure was modeled after the Young Pioneers Organization of the Soviet Union.

YPC had its own charter document. The first three clauses of the document spell out the purpose of this group:

1. Our founder and leader: Chinese Communist Party. The Party entrusted the direct leadership of Chinese Communist Youth League to lead our team.
2. The nature of our team: It is a mass organization of Chinese children. It teaches Chinese children about Communism. It exists to build a communist reserve for the future.
3. Our team goal: Uniting and educating children. Teach children to follow the lead of the Communist party. Teach children to love our motherland; love our people; love hard labor; protect public property; study hard; participate in physical exercise. Determine to become qualified personnel and contribute to build Communism with Chinese characteristic; become successors to the cause of Communism.[24]

Basically, YPC is an organization the Communist Party used to groom its heirs from a very young age. It had its own red flag. The color red symbolizes the blood shed by revolution martyrs. The five-pointed star in the middle symbolizes the leadership of the Communist Party, while the

---

[24] Young Pioneers of China

torch symbolizes brightness down the path of communism. Its members wore triangular red scarves.

Within each school, the Young Pioneers of China organization was structured like the military. The smallest unit was called a squad and was

Figure 16. The Young Pioneers flag (Commons, 2009)

made up of five to seven members. The leader of the squad wore a red scarf and a white shoulder badge with one red line in the center of the badge. The next level up was called a squadron, which normally consisted of several squads. The leader of the squadron wore a red scarf and a white shoulder badge with two red lines on the badge. The highest level was a battalion. Its leader wore a red scarf and a white shoulder badge with three red lines sewed on the badge. None of these student leaders were voted in; they were appointed by YPC counselors and teachers. Most students who took on leadership roles would later be part of the pool of candidates for the Youth League (for people 14–22) and later the Communist Party.

Applying for YPC membership was supposed to be a voluntary process. The YPC charter document said, "All children between six and fourteen years old, who are willing to participate in the Young Pioneers and abide by its Charter, can submit membership applications to the school. The Young Pioneer group will approve the applications." However, there was nothing voluntary about political indoctrination. Chinese elementary schools required their students to become members of the Young Pioneers group by the time they graduated. We were not only pressured to join, we also had to compete to be included in the first batch of admissions, because supposedly only the best students would be included in the first batch. I used the word "supposedly" because the best was not measured by grades alone.

The Young Pioneers group didn't make the application process very easy, especially for the first round of admissions. What was going on in the school was a miniature reflection of what was going on in the society in large. For example, your teacher would check what class categories your parents were. The privileged few youngsters who became YPC members in first grade were normally sons and daughters of the red classes such as Communist Party members or factory workers. Some teachers would accept bribes from parents in exchange for helping their children become Pioneers first, and some teachers made sure their own children were included in the first batch.

The moment the students in the first batch started wearing red scarves around their necks, they and everyone else knew that they were in a different class than the rest of us. They were politically advanced. All good things would happen to them. They would take the leadership roles such as class president and vice president. They would have the honor of carrying and raising the Chinese flag during our school ceremonies. If your parents were in one of the black classes, such as landlords, business owners, or counter-revolutionary rightists, your path to the YPC membership would be much harder. However, you still were pressured to submit a membership application year after year. Otherwise, the teacher would regard you as someone who lacked motivation to "demand political progress." Children from the black classes were rejected again and again until everyone else was admitted.

Besides the class categories, the Young Pioneers counselors would check how many times a student made sacrifices for other people, how many good deeds he or she did, and whether he or she worked hard during school organized physical labor. The ultimate role model of self-sacrifice was a solider named Lei Feng (18 December 1940–15 August 1962). It was said that he did many good deeds during his short life, such as returning wallets to their rightful owners, helping elders to cross the street, never buying any new clothes and sewing patches to his old clothes by himself, donating his savings to other people in need, etc. Most importantly, he demonstrated utterly unconditional devotion to the Communist Party and Chairman Mao. How did people know about all these good deeds that Lei Feng carried out? Supposedly, he kept a very detailed diary that documented his thoughts and deeds. It was said that he died at a young age while trying to save someone during a flood. After his death, his diary was "discovered," and people found out what a selfless man he was.

Chairman Mao wasted no time; he kicked off a propaganda campaign that asked the entire population to follow Lei Feng's example of self-sacrifice. Excerpts from Lei Feng's diary were published in newspapers and in our textbooks and read out loud on radios and at public gatherings. No one dared question whether this person actually existed or whether any of his good deeds were true.

The discovery of Lei Feng's diary prompted schoolteachers to demand their students keep diaries also. This practice continued for a long time after Lei Feng's death. The idea was that if Lei Feng did it, so should everyone else. My sister and brother had to do it, and so did I. We had to submit our diaries for our teacher's review on a weekly basis. We were expected to use the diaries to report our good deeds.

The weekly diary writing and reviewing became a real nuisance, because opportunities to do the kind of good deeds Lei Feng performed didn't come very often. I remember that, for one week, almost everyone in the class except me reported that he or she returned a missing wallet to its rightful owner. One had to wonder if there were really that many missing wallets around.

The ironic thing was that the heavy campaign on pushing everyone to follow the footsteps of this virtuous model actually forced youngsters to lie. My parents taught me to be an honest person. My father always said that the only way to live freely is not to tell a lie. Yet I wasn't rewarded for my honesty. Year after year, I submitted applications for the membership of the Young Pioneers Organization. Year after year, I was denied on the basis that I didn't do enough good deeds. I was definitely not in the first batch, and that was hard on my young psyche. Even though I was the top student in my class based on grades, I was humiliated. The counselor kept telling me not to put too much emphasis on studying, and instead to demonstrate more self-sacrifice for others.

My parents had different opinions on that. They never discounted any physical labor, but they told me to put my studies first. They were less concerned about my membership in the Young Pioneer Organization. They never bothered to join the Communist Party, although their stubbornness definitely hurt their careers. My parents would rather work hard and earn an honest living than act falsely, even if it meant they wouldn't see a penny's raise in their salaries. They didn't believe in selling their souls for a better life.

I initially was frustrated with my parents. I thought they didn't understand the kind of pressure that I had to endure when more and more of my classmates became YPC members and enjoyed the privilege of wearing the red scarf. My class was increasingly divided by the haves and have nots. Like any nine-year-old kid, I wanted to be like others. I craved conformity. Lacking the red scarf hurt my ambitions. I was always the class representative for the Chinese literature class. I really wanted to become a class president, but my teacher wouldn't appoint me unless I became a member of the Young Pioneers organization. I made the mistake of disclosing my desire for the class presidency in one of the weekly diaries. I naively thought that I should tell the truth in my diary.

The teacher made me read my diary in front of the rest of class. I was embarrassed when my secret wish became public. She made an example out of me by pointing out that "Ambition like this is dangerous. It is more honorable to desire to be people's servant first. You need to demonstrate that you are willing and ready to sacrifice for other people. Before you can become an YPC member, you have to pass some rigorous tests." To fight back tears, I bit my lips so hard I could taste blood.

I went home that day and told my parents what had happened. They looked at each other and let out a long sigh. My father held my hands and said, "There is nothing wrong with having ambitions. If you don't set a goal, how do you know where you are going? Just keep your thoughts to yourself, okay?"

I nodded. From then on, I didn't share my true thoughts in my weekly diary. Instead, I described weather and activities, but refrained from giving my opinions. I learned my first tough lesson in life.

When the YPC counselor asked me to be ready for rigorous tests of my resolve for the YPC membership, I thought she meant a written test, and I was pretty confident that I could excel at any test and thereby wash off this humiliation. However, it turned out that she meant a different test. When it was time for her to hand out assignments for school cleaning again, she announced that she was seeking volunteers for the dirtiest work—i.e. cleaning public restrooms. She kept looking at those of us who were applying for the YPC memberships. I knew she wanted one of us to do it, but it would come out better if we "volunteered" than if she asked directly. I couldn't do it. Our public restroom was beyond disgusting. Fortunately, someone else whose YPC application had also been rejected several times raised his hand to take on this difficult task. I pretended that I didn't notice our teacher's disappointed look toward me. Of course, my application to YPC was denied again right after.

My quest for progress was finally answered when I was in fourth grade. After 70% of my class wore red scarves, my application was finally approved. As always, the new member ceremony took place on the day of the Qing Ming Festival. Qing Ming Festival is a traditional Chinese holiday when Chinese people visit the graves of their ancestors and dead relatives to pay tribute and ask for blessings. Since the Communist Party took over China, paying tribute to revolutionary martyrs replaced the traditional practice of visiting family burial grounds. The date of Qing Ming is based on the Chinese lunar calendar. It usually falls around late March or early April.

I remember the day when I became an YPC member was a chilly day, but we had to wear the typical uniform of white shirts and blue pants. I guess that was another way to test our commitment to the cause. No one dared to sneeze or utter any words about the cold.

The Young Pioneers new members' ceremony took place at a revolutionary martyrs' burial ground. An old war hero gave us a lecture about the sacrifice revolutionary heroes made in order to liberate the repressed public. He recounted how miserable lives were before 1949 and how fortunate we were to grow up in Communist China. It was the same type of speech we heard year after year.

When it was time to take the oath, we saluted the Young Pioneers' flag by raising our right hands above our heads, with our fingers together and palms facing downwards. This gesture was supposed to symbolize the interests of the People supersede all of our individual needs.

The leader of the organization's battalion level led us in the oath. He shouted, "Be prepared to struggle for the cause of communism!" We shouted back, "Always be prepared!" Some existing YPC members presented us red scarves and helped us to tie them around our necks. Afterward, all new members, including me, took the following pledge:

I am a member of the Young Pioneers of China. Under the Flag of
the Young Pioneers, I promise that: I love the Communist Party of
China, the motherland, and the people; I will study well and keep
myself fit and prepare for: contributing my effort to the cause of
communism.

After the pledge, we sang the song "We are the Heirs of Communism."
Once we became members, we were required to wear the red scarf every
day. One day, one of my friends forgot her red scarf at home. The teacher
criticized her in front of everyone. Her face turned red and she started
sobbing. The teacher made her go back home to retrieve it. Since she lived
quite far from our school, she missed a half day of classes. But to our
teacher, it was more important for her to remember the scarf than not to
miss class. This was a typical communist technique of "Kill a chicken to
scare monkeys," which means punishing one to scare the others. We all
worried we might forget our red scarves and suffer the same humiliation.
Every night before I went to bed, I folded my red scarf in a neat triangle
and laid it right next to my pillow so I wouldn't forget it.

The red scarf that I had craved for so long didn't bring me the kind of
joy that I had dreamed of. Our teacher never appointed me class
president.

Food for Thought

My experience with the Young Pioneer Organization showed how far the Chinese
totalitarian regime would go to enforce thought control. Even children were not
spared. From a young age, we learned that the only right way to think was the
way sanctioned by the government. As John F. Kennedy pointed out,
"Conformity is the jailer of freedom and the enemy of growth."

It is disturbing how much the socialist ideology emphasizes the virtue of self-
sacrifice. Mao promoted selflessness and self-sacrifice through a mass campaign
of the make-believe example of Lei Feng. But the real motive of his campaign
was selfish, because communism was founded upon the belief that an individual
must sacrifice for the collective in order to achieve the common good.
Government requirements always took precedence over individual preference.
Therefore, the more people believed in self-sacrifice, the more people were
willing to suppress individualism, the easier it was for the state to abolish private

property rights and replace them with collective rights and state ownership of resources.

Of course, leaders of such a society were conveniently exempted from making any sacrifice.

In spite of his relentless campaign promoting virtues such as selflessness and self-sacrifice, Mao didn't get virtuous people because he took choice away. As a consequence of his totalitarian regime, even young kids learned to lie. That is not surprising, since communism is a system that rewards loyalty, not virtue.

Thomas Aquinas said, "Law cannot create virtuous men. The main thing in virtue is choice." No one should be forced into self-sacrifice. No one should feel morally entitled to the fruits of other people's labor. Free societies that recognize and protect individual rights and property rights are the societies whose people are most generous. Is it any wonder that American people are the most generous people in the world?

America is the richest and most powerful country in the world because it was founded on the faith in individuals' abilities to make the best out of themselves. Samuel Adams said, "It does not take a majority to prevail . . . but rather an irate, tireless minority, keen on setting brushfires of freedom in the minds of men." The minority in this sense is not people with a certain skin color or ethnicity, but people who hold different ideas. As Ayn Rand said, "The smallest minority is the individual." Free market capitalism will always triumph over socialism and communism because it is the only system that recognizes and protects individual rights.

CHAPTER 10

From Zigong to Wuhan

When my father published his first translated article, none of us realized it would mark a great transition in his life. Shortly after, he was invited to attend an engineering conference in Shijiazhuang, an industrial city in the northeast of China that is not too far from his hometown. Since I had never met my grandparents and great-grandparents, my father decided to take me with him. The plan was to drop me off with my grandparents while he was at the conference. Afterwards, he would come by to pick me up.

This was my first trip outside of Zigong and also my first time riding a train. My sister and brother were jealous. Since it would be an all-day train ride, my father and I stayed in the sleeping section of the train. It had rows of three-level bunk beds. Each bed was so tiny that even one person could hardly feel comfortable. To save money, my father booked only one bed. He let me sleep through the night while he sat next to me.

We arrived at Shijiazhuang the next day. He took me to a restaurant. I had never been to a restaurant before. He found an empty square table and set me down. There was no menu. Today's specials were written on a piece of paper outside the kitchen. He ordered steamed fish and two bowls of rice. When the fish was brought to the table, its mouth was still moving. The fish was covered by golden sauce and all kinds of spices, such as ginger, green onion, and red pepper. The sauce was so thick it dripped from the fish to the edges of the plate. It smelled so good that I swore I could just melt in its aroma. Oh, it was the most delicious thing I had ever had. My father and I, probably mostly I, inhaled every piece of the fish. Even today, I can still remember its taste.

After dinner, my father took me to the hotel. Upon examining our paperwork, the front desk staff led us into a big room. It was not a bedroom, as I had imagined, but rather a room about the size of a dining hall. There was a long platform on each side of the room, one side for men and the other side for women. My father told me that these platforms were called "kang." In northern China, people didn't sleep in beds; they slept on kang. A kang was a platform mostly made of bricks or fired clay. The center of the kang was like a chimney flue. It channeled the heat generated from cooking fires in an adjacent kitchen. This was an energy-efficient design, as the heat from cooking could keep the kang warm in winter — and northern China could get very cold.

We didn't have our own kang. Instead, I shared one with at least ten other women. Thank goodness, each of us at least had our own pillow and cover. But the kang was so crowded that it was difficult to turn. Every time I turned, I either saw the back of someone's head or found myself face to face with a stranger. The kang felt hard on my back. The woman next to me snored loudly. It took me quite a while to fall asleep.

I dreamed of the fish dish again.

The next day, my father and I rode a bus for several hours from Shijiazhuang to his village. When we got off the bus, we saw my uncle Yulun and my grandpa waiting for us at the bus station. They came with a wooden cart pulled by a skinny ox. The cart would be our ride. Uncle Yulun put our luggage on the cart. My father put me in the cart first and then he and Grandpa climbed in. Uncle Yulun sat at the front as our driver. The ox walked very slowly. I remember it had a little bell hanging around his neck. The bell sang with every step. I don't know how long our journey lasted because I dozed off to the rhythm of the ox cart.

That trip was the first time I met my father's side of family: great-grandparents, grandparents, uncles, aunties, and cousins. Since half the village shared our family name, I quickly lost track of who was who. But everyone knew who I was, because I was the first city girl they had met. Like my parents, my grandparents didn't spoil me much. Everyone in the household had to work, including my 80-year-old great-grandfather. My great-grandmother was the only one who didn't have to work in the field, because she had bound feet and could barely walk. Foot-binding, which traditionally had made Chinese women suffer for centuries, was banned by the communist government since 1949. So there is at least one good thing coming out of the revolution.

But my great-grandmother didn't sit idle at home; she kept herself busying by raising chickens and feeding pigs. Each day, when everyone else went to the fields, they took me along. My aunties showed me how to pick cotton flowers from the hard cotton shells without getting my finger sliced.

Young kids, like my cousins and me, were responsible for picking up anything that could fuel the kitchen stoves, such as dry grass and tree branches in the fields. Most people in the village were too poor to afford coal. They didn't even know about natural gas. The smoke from burning dry grass and tree branches made Grandma cough a lot. All I could do was to pat her back when she coughed and hope that she would feel better. I wished she had natural gas as cooking fuel, like we did in Zigong.

There was no electricity in the village either. At night, people either burn candles or lit oil lamps. Since both candles and oil cost money, most people just went to bed right after dinner. When I was in Zigong, I had gotten used to reading books before I went to bed. But I gave it up at my grandparent's house.

Life in the village was hard. I missed my mother and everyone back in Zigong. In my young heart, for the first time, I realized that my life in Zigong was privileged compared to what my relatives had to endure in the village. I didn't know if my father intended to teach me a life lesson, but I learned one. I stayed with my grandparents for a week, until my father finished his business and came to pick me up. When we went back to Zigong, I wasn't the same eight-year-old girl as before.

Our trip to Shijiazhuang not only introduced me to the outside world for the very first time, it also paved a new career path for my father. He told us that before his trip to Shijiazhuang, he was like a frog living at the bottom of a well. He thought the sky was only as big as the opening of the well. After his trip to Shijiazhuang, he realized that Zigong and even the Sichuan province were culturally isolated and economically backward compared to the east coast of China. I had to agree with him when my mother took me to visit her side of the family in Wuhan a year later. We took a boat ride along the Yangtze River. Wuhan was a much bigger and more developed city than Zigong. I felt like a country bumpkin in Wuhan.

My father started collecting any English industrial journals he could get his hands on. After dinner each day, he sat by his desk with an English-Chinese dictionary in hand, working on translating articles. The rest of us sat by our dining table, either working on our homework or working on additional study materials that my mother assigned us. My father's drive for success set a good example without him having to say anything. None of us wanted to go to sleep before he did.

Over the next two years, my father translated another twenty some English articles. Gradually, he started gaining recognition within the industry, and more and more conferences invited him to speak. Frequent trips outside of Zigong made Father more determined than ever to move out of Sichuan.

Under the strict household registration system, moving was difficult in China. However, my father was persistent. It helped that China had a shortage of people who understood English and chemical engineering. An opportunity finally came. Two institutes, one located in Qingdao, Shangdong province, and another one located in Wuhan, Hubei province, extended olive branches to my father. He initially preferred the institute in Qiangdao, because it was closer to his hometown. But this institute told him that the city of Qingdao issued very limited household registration quotas for new migrants. He would have to be the first one to move. The rest of us might have to wait for at least another year. The institute also couldn't guarantee a job for my mother. Overall, it was not a very appealing offer for him so he had to decline it.

The institute from Wuhan initially indicated similar challenges for moving our household registrations to Wuhan, due to their strict quota. I guess their need for an expert who knew a foreign language was pressing enough that eventually it was worked out, so all of us were guaranteed residency in Wuhan.

My mother was ecstatic. She had never dreamed that she could move back to her hometown. Seventeen years before, she had been forced to move to Zigong as an 18-year-old young woman with one suitcase. Now, she would move back home with a family of her own. It felt like a miracle. The last three weeks before we left Zigong, we never cooked dinner. My parents' friends, especially patients my mother had treated over the years, took turns treating us.

My Chinese literature teacher announced to my class that I was moving. I received many gifts from my classmates. Most were something really small, like a piece of shell or a small notebook. I had a crush on one boy in my class before I understood what "crush" meant. Unlike schools in America, dating in schools in China was strictly forbidden. If either parents or teachers caught any sign of it, nobody would say it was cute. Instead, the students' parents would beat those unhealthy thoughts out of their children. Therefore, the boy I liked and I barely spoke to each other over the years. I had no idea whether he liked me or not. The day before we moved, I went to school and discovered that there were four notebooks in my drawer, all from him. Maybe this was him telling me that he liked me. For the first time in my young life, I felt incredibly happy and sad at the same time.

On the Chinese New Year's Eve in 1985, we packed our belongings and spent our last night in the hotel. All of us shared the same room, which had three bunk beds. I slept on one of the top ones. In the middle of night, I fell onto the floor and got a big bump on my forehead. My sister joked that I had to give Zigong's soil one last kiss goodbye.

We rode a train from Zigong to Chongqing. Chongqing was a big port on the Yangtze River. On the boat ride from Chongqing to Wuhan we had to sleep in bunk beds again. To prevent me from falling, my father tied ropes around the bed.

Since I had made this trip before with my mother, I volunteered to be our family tour guide. I didn't last very long as a tour guide, because I got a fever. When the boat passed the famous Three Gorges, my father had to carry me on his back to the deck so I could enjoy the scenery for the second time.

The Three Gorges is 120 miles long. It used to be the most scenic area along the Yangtze River. It was also a historically and culturally important location in China. Many settlements and archeological sites could be found along the way. I am always grateful that I was able to see it twice with my parents. Later, when the Three Gorges Dam was built in 2012, the dam flooded many of these archeological and cultural sites and displaced some 1.3 million people. The scenery at the Three Gorges was altered forever. Future generations will never have the chance to see it. It was said that Mao was the one who had the vision of building the Three Gorges Dam. Many scientists, engineers and archeologists came out against the dam project, but all of them lost to a dead dictator.

When we moved to Wuhan, it already had close to ten million people. It was probably five times larger than Zigong. In Zigong, we rarely took the bus, because the town was smaller but densely populated, we could walk practically everywhere. Zigong had small town charm, while Wuhan, like all big cities, was crowded and noisy everywhere I went. I couldn't go anywhere without taking the bus, but it was always a physical struggle to squeeze myself onto an overcrowded bus. I never mastered the physical skill even till the day I left.

Figure 17. My father and me at a park in Wuhan

The new institute that my father worked for was a large, state-run organization. It had a tall and wide iron front gate with an armed guard twenty-four hours a day, seven days a week. It was surrounded by brick walls that separated it from the outside world. Inside the walls, it was its own universe. Like many large, state-run organizations in China, this institute was made up of two main sections: the work section and residential section. The two sections were separated by another wall and another iron gate. The work section consisted of several office buildings, and my father worked in one of those buildings.

It also had rows of gray apartment buildings. Our new home was on the third floor of one of those buildings, so my parents had less than a five minute commute. The residential area had its own clinic and cafeteria. The clinic was much bigger than the one in Zigong. My mother worked as one of the doctors there.

We had three bedrooms, a living room, and, for the first time, a kitchen and toilet inside our apartment. We had never before had so much space in our lives. My parents got their own bedroom, as did my brother. My sister and I shared a bedroom, but she was already a high school senior, and I knew that bedroom was mine once she was off to college. If I'd ever had any doubt whether we should've moved to Wuhan, the new apartment convinced me that my father was right.

Things were going well for my parents. They got their first raises in seventeen years as part of the move. Their salaries were still low—together no more than twenty dollars per month—but that was double what they had made in Zigong.

Similar to many other state run organizations, the institute kept its employees' salaries low, but handed out household stuffs as part of employee benefits. Over the years, my parents brought home work units' handouts, such as toilet paper, soaps, and shampoo. Since my father traveled for business quite a bit, the institute ordered a new outfit for him. Gone was the black-and-gray Mao suit; along came a navy blue Western-style suit and tie. It was funny to watch my father learn to tie a tie for the first time.

Another benefit the institute provided its employees and their families was hot water. No one had a hot water heater at home. Like everything else, when it was offered free, the supply was limited. Free hot water was supplied on a limited schedule 6–7:30 a.m. and 5–6 p.m. Therefore, one of our new house chores was to join long lines of people twice a day and carry hot water back in thermoses.

A limited hot water supply also meant that taking a bath at home was a challenge. Another added employee benefit was a communal shower house run by the institute. A hot shower was not free, so my parents had to buy tickets. Since men and women had to use the same communal shower house, it opened to women only on Monday, Wednesday, and Friday, and to men the rest of the week. I never liked taking a communal shower, because I often had to share a showerhead with three or four other totally naked women. There were always more women than showerheads, so petty fights broke out among bunches of naked women all the time. It was the most bizarre things to witness. Nevertheless, my mother kept telling me that not all organizations provided hot showers, so the communal shower was a great benefit. I didn't believe her until teachers at my new school asked me if my parents could secure some shower tickets for them.

After we settled down in our new apartment, we begged our parents to buy a TV. However, when the first summer in Wuhan came along, none of us was prepared when the heat and humidity pushed the temperature to over 100 degrees for weeks on end. The institute allocated about 100 pounds of fresh watermelons to each household. We didn't have a refrigerator, so most water melons we received went bad pretty quickly. My parents hated to waste food more than anything. Therefore, they vetoed our plea for a TV and decided that we should buy a fridge first. To save money for it, we agreed that except absolute essentials, we wouldn't buy anything new for a year—no new clothes or shoes. My mother also cut back on our food budget. We had almost nothing but home-made pickled vegetables with pig fat for dinner until we saved enough money for a fridge.

Figure 18. Mom standing next to our first refrigerator

Buying appliances in China was not just a money issue. We also needed a government-issued coupon. Unlike American coupons, the Chinese coupon wasn't for saving money but for controlling demand when supply was limited. Not every household got a coupon, so coupons for the most demanded items were traded in the black market like a shadow currency. My mother eventually got one from a friend's friend who worked for a refrigerator manufacturer. Even with both money and coupon in hands, we had to stand in a long line until it was our turn. We couldn't choose which refrigerator we wanted. There was only one size and color available. If we said no, 100 other people would be more than happy to take our fridge home. So we agreed to pick the first one we saw in the store. Later, after it was delivered to our home, my parents put it at the most visible place in the living room. This was the most expensive thing we had ever owned. Because of air pollution, even things inside a house got dusty easily. So my mother made a cover for the new fridge. As a matter of fact, over the years, she made covers for every appliance we bought, including a black-and-white TV.

By and large, our lives had materially improved since we had moved to Wuhan.

I don't know how long it took the rest of my family to adjust to life in Wuhan. I embraced my new life wholeheartedly. What wasn't to like? New place, new people, new apartment, and new school. Even our photos were no longer black and white. We had color photos for the first time. People's clothes became more colorful in real life, too. I noticed that my mother stopped complaining about her naturally curly hair. She actually got a set of curlers to make her hair more curly. She also started to wear shoes with small heels. As far as I remembered, when we had lived in Zigong, she always wore flat, black cotton cloth shoes. I don't know if those were her decision or those were the only shoes available. I thought she looked much prettier with curly hair and heeled shoes.

After we moved to Wuhan, not only our personal lives changed; there were many visible changes throughout the country. We started to hear leaders talk more about economic reforms, less about class struggles. Deng Xiao Peng said something very shocking: "It is okay to get rich." Several years back, the same Communist Party proclaimed that "To be poor is glorious." Chinese people were used to being poor and became fearful if they were perceived to live a better life than their neighbors. Now, as the government changed its slogans, many people were at a loss. They didn't know how to interpret what the government really meant, and if the new slogans were a trap to catch hidden capitalist enemies lucky enough have escaped previous political campaigns.

Even with economic reforms, Chinese government had total control of every aspect of a person's life: housing, food rations, licensing for marriage and child birth, movement, etc. In exchange, anyone who held a job with either the government or a state-owned enterprise had guaranteed job security as well as a steady income and benefits. This arrangement was called the "iron rice bowl." After the initial success of the household responsibility system in agriculture, the Chinese government gradually pushed a similar concept onto the state-owned enterprise.

Some brave souls decided to test the water. They smashed their iron rice bowls by quitting their jobs at state enterprises and starting small businesses. This move was nicknamed "go to the sea." That was very descriptive, since many people viewed the ocean as unpredictable and dangerous.

We began to see more and more small shops, such as barber shops, street vendors and restaurants, pop up outside the cast iron gate of the institute where we lived. They represented what the state called the "individual economy." Similar economic changes were taking place elsewhere in China. For us, the consumers, we had something we never had before: choice. We could choose to go to one barber shop instead of the other. When there was competition, we got better service at a lower price.

Soon, the newspaper reported that some barbers and street vendors were making more money than doctors and scientists did. This caused a big debate within the Chinese society. Many state employees and intellectuals hadn't seen a salary increase in years. It hurt their pride to learn that some businessmen with elementary school educations could do better financially than they. They remembered that, not so long ago, private business owners were ruthlessly persecuted by the communist government. People were asking a soul-searching question: should someone who sells boiled eggs on the street make more money than a scientist who develops nuclear weapons?

With the economic and political change, there were visible signs of cultural change. In the past, the entirety of China had one TV station — Center China Television Station (CCTV) — run by the central government. When we moved to Wuhan, we learned that there were three TV stations available; the provincial government and the city government operated their own stations in addition to CCTV. We only turned on CCTV for hardcore news, because the majority of their other programming was dull. Most of the revolutionary movies or TV series it showed were boring, and their storylines followed the same predictable formulas. The good guy was always a communist, and, no matter how many gunshots he received or how badly he was tortured, he never died — just like James Bond, except I didn't know anything about James Bond then. The bad guys were always landlords, capitalists, spies, or some other kind of exploiters. Good guys were good looking and bad guys were ugly.

Most of us liked the TV station run by the city government. It was less rigid and had better programming. For example, it showed TV series from Hong Kong and Taiwan. Of course, these series were a decade old. The TV series from Hong Kong were adapted from books written by the wildly popular Hong Kong author Louis Cha Leung-yung. They were mostly about fictional martial arts heroes. The TV series from Taiwan were adapted from books written by Chiung Yao, a popular romance writer from Taiwan. In these shows, even the bad guys were very good looking. Their martial arts movements were rudimentary compared to today's movies, but we were addicted to watching them because the plots were entertaining: the perceived good guy tended to be the most evil person in the end and the seemingly bad guys were lovable. There was definitely no politics involved. These shows didn't share the seriousness of TV series and movies made in mainland China.

Gradually, some brave young people started to imitate pop stars from Hong Kong and Taiwan by growing long hair, wearing pants with big flares, and walking around the downtown commercial district with big boom boxes in their hands. Loud pop songs from Hong Kong and Taiwan could be heard several blocks away. These young people were referred to as hooligans, and my parents warned me to stay away from them. They were considered a disgrace to society. Many of them were offspring of the youth who'd been forced to migrate to the countryside decades earlier. Now, they either had no household registration—so they couldn't get any food rationing—or they had household registration but were so poorly educated that they couldn't find any meaningful jobs. This was my first time to encounter the anti-cultural bad boy type. Years later, when I watched John Travolta's movie *Saturday Night Fever*, he reminded me of those young Chinese men.

For years, Chinese people were told to hate America and that the United States was responsible for all the evil in the world. My mother often reminded me to clean up my bowl at the dinner table because poor kids in America were starving. She wasn't trying to lie to me; that was what the Chinese government had told us for years.

When I was in the ninth grade, the city TV station started showing old Disney cartoons for half an hour each day. These were early cartoons made in the 30s and 40s. Most of them were black and white and had minimal dialogue. If we were culturally a decade behind Hong Kong and Taiwan, we were definitely four or five decade behind the Western culture. Still, it was a refreshing experience to watch these Disney cartoons, because I had never seen anything like them before. Mickey Mouse's and Donald Duck's uniquely American style of humor, optimism, and harmless silliness were like fresh air. Watching a Disney cartoon for half an hour each day became the happiest time in my life. I couldn't help thinking that a country that produced Mickey and Donald must be a really happy place.

Food for Thought

One life lesson that I learned from my father was never to let circumstance make decisions for you.   There is no doubt that the circumstances and the environments we are in have great influence on our lives. But ultimately, how our lives turn out largely rests on our own actions. When a person focuses first and foremost on changing himself, usually he ends up changing the situation he's in.   Therefore, instead of blaming the circumstances you are in, ask yourself: What changes can I make for myself? Maya Angelou said, "If you don't like something, change it. If you can't change it, change your attitude."

It is worth pointing out that China's economic reforms started in a grassroots fashion rather than a top-down command. Those village leaders in Anhui put their lives on the line when they decided to implement measures to pull their villagers and themselves out of misery. Their experiences show that people can improve their standard of living if there is less government control, more individual rights. For those who argue for more government intervention in the United States, I recommend the book *How China Became Capitalist* by Ronald Coase and Ning Wang. This wonderful book provides a strong case that China's economic resurgence in recent decades was mostly caused by political leaders seeing the private sector blooming without state help and having the good sense to keep the state somewhat out of the way.

While China's economy is improved by some free market elements, the economies of America and Western Europe are being transformed by some doses of socialist central command elements, such as increases in regulations. Ludwig von Mises pointed out that "Economics is not about goods and services; it is about human choice and action."

The transformation in China showed that ordinary people can improve their lives even with limited freedom of choice. The question for people in the U.S. is: Why are Americans going backwards and allowing the state to take more command and control of economic activities?

CHAPTER 11

Summer Awakening

Do you suppose a girl should eat less than a boy? You may think that is a crazy question. Yet not so long ago, China's food ration policy was based on the assumption that a girl should eat less than a boy.

Growing up, we had food stamps for essentials such as rice, cooking oils, meat, and eggs. For the same aged boy and girl, a boy would get about four more pounds of rice on a monthly basis. My Chinese name happens to be a common boy's name. Therefore, I received the amount of rice for a boy. Even with this extra rice, I was always hungry. When I was 15, a policeman came to our house for an inspection. In China, this kind of unannounced inspection was routine and common. Once he realized I was girl, he ordered me to pay the government back. For the next couple of years, my whole family had to go on a diet in order to save enough food stamps to pay the government back. This incident left a profound impact on my life. For the first time, I started questioning if there was any validity in China's governmental system.

In the late 1980s, the Chinese government granted us a little more economic freedom than we'd had in the past, but it didn't let go of thought control, especially the early political indoctrination of Chinese youth. Chinese children from six to fourteen years old are required to join the Young Pioneers of China (YPC). That was why I was a member of the YPC. When I was in high school, there was another political organization, called the Communist Youth League (CYL), which targeted Chinese youth from fourteen to twenty-two years old. CYL membership is more selective than the YPC because the CYL provides a pool of candidates for the Communist Party. Therefore, only about a third of the Young Pioneers became members of the Communist Youth League.

The CYL only admits the elite members of each class. The first batch of members for the CYL is naturally those who took leadership roles in the YPC. They do not necessarily have the best grades (their grades have to be at least above average), but they all come from good families. For example, they are likely to be the offspring of current Communist Party members or revolutionary martyrs. They have to prove that they are loyal to the communist cause. It is ironic that the communist regime advocates absolute equality in its slogans but heavily favor the elites in practice. Of course, there is always a price to pay for elite membership. CYL has tight control over its members. On a biweekly basis, all members have to attend secret political study sessions.

Even though I was one of the top students in my class, I told my parents that I had neither the desire nor the motivation to become a Communist Youth League member. My experience with the Young Pioneers had left a scar on my psyche. In addition, the whole incident of being forced to return extra food stamps only because I was girl really upset me. Who other than I should decide how much I should eat? I was afraid to say it out loud, but I started to doubt some of the political teachings I received.

My aversion to the Youth League didn't upset my parents. They never joined the Youth League or the Communist Party. But they both worked for Communist Party members in their work units, members who had a lot of political savvy but little technical knowledge. My parents despised people who use political slogans to hide their ignorance. My parents have a strong conviction that everyone should make an honest living based on knowledge and skill. I was grateful towards my parents for not pressuring me to join the Youth League, even though they knew that I probably would have a better career if I did.

Although I wasn't interested in the Youth League, plenty of other young people throughout China were eager to submit their applications and become members. According to the China Daily News, the Communist Youth League of China has a total of 90 million members, as of the end of 2012. It is a powerful organization and has contributed a number of top leaders to the Communist Party and the government of the

People's Republic of China.   The first Youth League faction was represented by Hu Yaobang, general secretary (1980–87) and chairman (1981–82) of the Chinese Communist Party.

Hu was promoted to his leadership positions by Deng Xiaoping and carried out a series of political and economic reforms in the 1980s under Deng's guidance.   One of his political reform initiatives was to encourage intellectuals to speak up about some of the wrongdoings under Mao's Cultural Revolution and propose a more sensible approach to move the country forward.   With his support, a group of intellectuals advocated that China should learn from Western civilization: rule of law, free and open markets, and more personal freedom.   Of course, ideas such as these couldn't be expressed in China openly and directly; they had to be communicated in subtext and discreetly.

In order to do this, some reform-minded intellectuals produced a documentary TV series to explore the historical and cultural influence of the Yangtze River.   The Yangtze is the longest river in China and had provided water and natural resources that supported generations of Chinese people for thousands of years.   It is called the mother river of China and was a symbol of Chinese civilization.   The historical influence of Yangtze River was really a reflection on Chinese history.   The TV series discussed the cause of China's humiliating contemporary history since the first Opium war in 1840.   It contrasted China's isolation and backwardness in the last 100 years with the development of science and the social progress brought on by the Industrial Revolution in the West.   The TV series seemed to think that the Europeans' command of oceans and willingness to explore the unknown contributed to their world domination.   It referred to the West as an ocean-based civilization.   In contrast, the TV series labeled China as a land-based civilization.   China's thousands of years history only produced one great seaman—Zhenhe, who reached the African coast in the early 1400s.   After Zhenhe, Chinese rulers stopped supporting exploration and turned inward.   The TV series argued that that was when China started to decline and eventually led to humiliating defeat after defeat in the last 100 years, from 1840 to 1949.   At the end of the TV series, the announcer asked the audience if China should learn from the West and try to become a more ocean-based civilization. Should we as a country be open to more change?

This TV documentary was unlike anything we had seen before.   It became widely popular. The theme song from the show also became popular in China in the late 80s and early 90s. In every group singing contest or performance, often more than one group would choose to sing it.

My Chinese literature teacher, Ms. Peng, was a devoted fan of the TV series. She asked us to watch it and report our thoughts through our weekly diaries. At this time, we were still required to submit weekly diaries to a teacher so she could examine our thoughts. It was peculiar that Ms. Peng was inspired by the liberal message from the TV series on the one hand, but on the other hand, didn't find anything wrong with requiring us to share our private thoughts.

The TV series was obviously created to support Chinese leader Hu's reform message. However, Hu's political opponents, who opposed political and economic reform from the beginning, were offended by the TV series' glowing admiration for Western civilization. They blamed Hu for his bourgeois reforms and forced him to resign from his Communist Party Secretary post in 1987. Hu was replaced by Zhao Ziyang, who turned out to be another reform-minded leader. Hu himself, however, disappeared from the public eye.

Looking back, 1986 to 1989 was probably the most liberal period in China's history since the founding of communist China in 1949. We never heard anything about Hu again until 1989, when he passed away in April. Coincidentally, he died right around the Qingming holiday, a traditional Chinese holiday when people pay tribute to their deceased loved ones. Many ordinary Chinese people took to the street to pay tribute for Hu's death. Gradually, mourning for Hu turned into a movement calling on the Chinese government to grant people more freedom and to apply meaningful anticorruption measures. Peaceful demonstrators, mostly students, started occupying Beijing's Tiananmen Square.

During the early stage of the movement, the central government under the Communist Party secretary Zhao Zhiyang showed a certain level of tolerance. China Central TV gave a relatively fair broadcasting coverage of daily activities on the square. Students from the Central Art Institute built a Chinese version of the Statue of Liberty in the middle of the Tiananmen Square. They also read out a translated version of the America's Declaration of Independence. Like millions of Chinese people, it was my first time to hear those magnificent words of the Declaration: "We hold these truths to be self-evident, that all men are created equal, that they are endowed by their Creator with certain unalienable Rights, that among these are Life, Liberty and the pursuit of Happiness." These principles were very different from those we were used to hearing and how we were taught.

For 2000 years, Chinese people followed the moral principles and social orders established by Confucian teaching: The individual is insignificant and his proper role is to serve the almighty state's wishes. Mao's Cultural Revolution campaign tried to erase Confucian teaching and influence from Chinese society. He proclaimed his goal was to create an egalitarian society. But his emphasis on class struggle and class hatred further segregated Chinese society into a privileged class vs. everyone else. Mao and the other Communist Party members emerged as the privileged class. They rose above the law. Everyone in China knew being a communist meant a good job, promotions, and a better life. Those who were not Party members were subject to extensive laws and regulations in every aspect of their lives. As George Orwell said in *Animal Farm*, "All animals are equal, but some animals are more equal than others."

Mao and his communist cadres created the most powerful state in China's history. Group needs took precedence over individual needs. The leadership made decisions on behalf of every Chinese person regarding how much food one could have, what one could wear, what one could study, whom one should work for, which social class one belonged to, even what thoughts one should have. In the entire country, all men had the same haircut; likewise the women. Everyone wore the identical outfit with the only choice being color-black, blue, or gray. Afraid of retribution, people buried their individualities and replaced them with conformity, from outerwear to inner thoughts. In the end, people became dispensable and negligible: Millions perished during Mao's countless political campaigns and the Great Famine caused by poor policies. The economic and political reforms in the 1980s brought Chinese people some relief, but their basic relationship with the state didn't change. It felt like the old Chinese saying: "You can put an old rice wine in a new bottle, but you won't be able to change its sour taste."

Hearing America's Declaration of Independence read out loud by students on TV awakened something deep in people's souls. The principles it conveyed had universal appeal. Throughout China, from big cities to small towns, more and more people, especially students, took to the streets to support the students on hunger strike in Beijing and demand deeper reform not only on an economic front, but also on a human rights front. People voluntarily donated money and food to the protestors. For a while, everyone was hopeful that some real political changes would happen.

Change did take place, but not the kind people hoped. Sensing that the government might be losing control, Deng once again showed his iron fist. Party secretary Zhao Zhiyang was dismissed and stripped of his official duties. He disappeared from China's political scene overnight — similar to what had happened to his predecessor, Hu. No explanation was given. People took the cue of shifting political winds. Zhao's photo was no longer on the front page of any newspaper. After that, the tone of CCTV's coverage on student protest changed to a negative one. Students in the Tiananmen Square were accused of being under foreign enemy's influence. Adults like my parents, who experienced many of the Chinese Communist Party's past political campaigns, sensed something terrible was about to happen.

On the fateful day of June 4th, we woke up to the news that Tiananmen Square was cleared up. CCTV acknowledged that Chinese military tanks had been sent to the square, but there was no official coverage of what exactly took place. We noticed something odd when we watched the CCTV news. The female anchor who read the prepared report seemed overly solemn and wore a black armband. Black is an ominous color in China, and it is normally associated with death. It was a Chinese custom to wear a black armband if someone in your family passed away. Before we could figure out what subtle message she was trying to send to the audience, she was replaced by a different anchor. She never appeared in public after that day. There were rumors about innocent people being killed, but the government insisted that no one died during the June 4th clean up. People who participated in the protests were quietly being persecuted. Some university students who graduated in the summer of 1989 were sent to work in remote areas as a punishment for their participation in the protests.

My Chinese literature teacher, Ms. Peng, stopped talking about the TV series on the Yangtze River. As a matter of fact, she never mentioned it again. The theme songs from the TV series were removed from our group singing competitions.

Since 1989, June 4th has become a sensitive subject in China. Every year, any reference to this day, the movement, or key players will cause trouble. As a 9th grader in 1989, I was too young to comprehend the historical significance of the events taking place that summer. For a while, though, the TV station stopped showing my favorite Disney cartoons. It was an outcome of the economic boycott. I didn't know what happened until years later, after I moved to the United States, when I saw footages and pictures shot by foreign journalists for the first time, including the Pulitzer winning photo of a young Chinese guy standing in front of rows of tanks.

If you haven't seen this "tank man" photo, I would encourage you to look it up online. When I first saw this photo, the young man in the picture seemed small and vulnerable. But his status grew when I realized that he was taking a stand against not just the tanks, but also the entire totalitarian regime. He was making a powerful statement to the regime: "You can crush me, but you do not own me, because I am a free man." His action made him a giant. If I could add a caption to this photo, I would choose: "Give me liberty or give me death."

The thirst for liberty is the same for Patrick Henry and this unknown young man, because "We are born this way." We are all born as free men with equally inalienable rights. For the man standing in front of the tank, the individual rights he was fighting for weren't recognized and protected by the Chinese government.

The events that took place in the summer of 1989 had different influences on different people. Some continued to fight the government for political rights and were punished; some sought refuges in foreign countries; some sought and obtained favors from the political system they had once fought in order to get rich quickly; many went on living as they had prior to 1989. As always, Chinese government-sanctioned history books glossed over the period, so many people who were born in the late 80s or early 90s had no idea that it ever took place.

One thing that changed for me was that I became interested in learning more about the West. My sister was a great influence on me. At that time, she was studying Ernest Hemingway's literature as part of her Master in Literature program. She encouraged me to read several of Hemingway's books in Chinese: *A Farewell to Arms, For Whom the Bell Tolls*, and, of course, *The Old Man and the Sea.* I was mesmerized by Hemingway's writing style and storytelling ability. I was especially touched by his book *The Old Man and the Sea,* because Santiago, the fisherman in the book, reminded me of my maternal grandfather, who had been a fisherman himself. It was the first book I read that was not about team effort or group accomplishment. Its emphasis on individual effort and what a strong willpower could do left an enormous impression on me. My sister told me that I wouldn't be able to fully appreciate Hemingway's writing until I read his work in English. I used to dislike English because my English teacher was boring. Now, I was more motivated and started to work hard on learning English. In the summer of 1989, I didn't have lofty ambitions of living in America someday. I merely had a feeling that I needed to be good at English. Someday, it might become a key to opening doors of opportunity.

Food for Thought

From 1949 to 1979, Chinese people were deliberately cut off from the outside world and lived in isolation. Government propaganda kept informing us we were lucky to live in communist China because people in the West, especially in America, were destitute as a result of exploitation by evil capitalists. Most of us believed this nonsense and lived through immense misery with total obedience because we had neither comparison nor alternative. We were told that being able to "eat bitterness," a Chinese slang term for suffering without complaining, was a great virtue.

However, the economic reforms in the 1980s allowed information to flow from the outside world and many of us had a rude awakening: people in the West didn't live in destitute situations; instead, we were the ones being exploited. There was a lot of soul searching regarding what went wrong and how we could change it. Some intellectuals turned to the United States, the richest and most powerful country in the world, for an answer.

The reason America is like a magnet, attracting the best and brightest around the world, is that it is a nation of moral meaning and the moral principles it was founded upon transcend culture and awaken something deep in people's souls. People who are thirsty for freedom claim these moral principles as their own, as if they are, as Abraham Lincoln said, "Blood of the blood, and flesh of the flesh, of the men who wrote that Declaration."

That is why Chinese students stood on Tiananmen Square and read out loud the Declaration of Independence.

While people in other parts of the world shed blood for individual rights, some people here in the United States have lost the kind of convictions the Declaration instilled, and they blame others for their misfortunes. They turn needs into demands, demands into rights, and rights into entitlements. It is understandable that some people want to exchange a little bit of liberty for safety, especially during difficult times. But this is a dangerous trajectory. If you accept that universal healthcare is good, what will stop the government from regulating what and how much you can eat like the Chinese government did? If you want the government to take over student loans, what will stop the government from telling you where you can live and work?

These are not outlandish assumptions. China's history has shown that absolute equality can only be achieved through brutal force, with millions dying along the way. The more the government power grows, the more inequality grows.

The founders of this country pledged their "lives, fortunes, and sacred honor" to establishing a constitutional republic based on protecting each individual's unalienable rights. More than 200 years ago, when Benjamin Franklin walked out the constitutional convention, he was asked what kind of government the founders had given us. His answer was, "A republic, if you can keep it." The question we ought to ask ourselves today is: "Are we doing the right things to keep it?"

CHAPTER 12

Study, Study, Study

After my family moved to Wuhan, my sister became a freshman at Hubei University. She lived in a dorm, so I didn't see her often. There was a high school right next to where we lived. My brother enrolled in the tenth grade, and I enrolled in seventh grade.

Going to junior high was exciting for me. There were about 200 students in seventh grade, so we were divided into four classes. Each class had 50 or so students, which was a typical class size in China. Students were assigned to classes based on their graduation test results from elementary school. Class One and Class Two were for advanced students. They were taught by the best teachers. Class Three was for mediocre students. Class Four was for students who had been designated as losers already at their young ages. Very few teachers cared if these students learned anything. Unlike American schools, in China, once students are assigned to a class, they will take all their subjects together throughout a school year.

I was assigned to Class One. Our curriculum for the seventh grade included Chinese literature, math, English, Chinese history, politics, music, and P.E. Teachers assigned class representatives for each subject. I was the class representative for Chinese literature because I always scored the highest on Chinese literature exams and the literature teacher, Ms. Peng, often read out loud my essays to the rest of the class. Our school day started at 7:30 a.m. There was a mandatory morning reading time from 7:30 to 8:00 a.m. The class representative of English and I took turns leading the rest of the class in reading assignments aloud. We were required to memorize them as part of the exams. After the mandatory reading session, the rest of our school day consisted of seven sessions: four sessions in the morning and three sessions in the afternoon. Each session was forty-five minutes long plus a ten minute break. Unlike high schools in the United States, in China, we didn't change classrooms between subjects. Everyone stayed in the same room for all subjects. Since we had a large classroom size, two students, usually a boy and a girl, would share a desk. We were not allowed to choose whom we wanted to sit next to. Seating arrangements were predetermined by our teacher.

Teacher historically has been a highly respected profession in Chinese. When a teacher walked in a classroom, we rose and bowed; when he left the classroom, we rose and bowed again. The Chinese style of teaching was heavily lecture based. We never raised our hands to ask our teachers any questions because we were not supposed to challenge authority. We could only talk during the class when a teacher asked one of us to answer a question. There were no bathroom breaks for anyone during class. We could only move when a teacher asked one or several us to demonstrate how to solve a problem on the blackboard. Otherwise, all we were supposed to do was to listen quietly and take notes. If a student was caught chitchatting, he would be asked to stand in the back of the classroom for the remainder of the class.

English wasn't my strong suit at the beginning. My first English teacher was a lady with very messy hair. She tried to teach us English with a British accent. The sound came out very funny. We did a lot of drills on letters, words, phrases, and grammar. They were repetitive and boring. Instead of paying attention to her, my friend and I spent our time guessing how many hair pins she used. We obviously had to do this discretely so we wouldn't end up standing at the back of the classroom. As I mentioned in a previous chapter, I didn't become interested in learning English until 1989, when I was ready to go to high school.

Another subject I didn't like in junior high was P.E. However, I did enjoy our school's annual track and field competition, mainly because we could stay outside all day and had no homework to worry about. Each class selected its best athletes to compete against the best athletes from other classes in the same grade. I wasn't very good at any track and field activities, so this was the only competition that I never took part in. However, I didn't sit idle either, because I was one of the cheerleaders.

Unlike American cheerleaders, I didn't wear a miniskirt, nor did I wave pompoms. That was not how Chinese students did cheerleading then. Instead, I wrote motivational short poems and sent them to the school announcers. They read them aloud to cheer our athletes up. I don't remember anything I wrote, but I do remember that I was highly productive and my poems were effective.

When I got into eighth grade, our seating arrangement had a significant change. Girls had to share desks with girls only, while boys had to share desks with boys. This new arrangement took place precisely at a time when we started to notice the opposite sex. Teenage flirtation was strictly forbidden in Chinese schools. If discovered, both students would be punished. There wasn't much time for young love anyway; we had a lot of exams. Our test scores, with the exception of weekly exams, were posted on the back wall of our classroom so everyone knew where everyone else stood. The most important exams were the finals at the end of the school year. Students who failed to pass them weren't allowed to move on to the next grade. Instead, they were required to retake the same grade for another school year and take the final exams again. When this happened, both the students and their parents felt a great deal of humiliation.

In eighth grade, physics and chemistry were added to our curriculum, and our afternoon sessions were increased to four. Our physics teacher was a handsome young man who'd just graduated from a teaching school. Many girls had a crush on him. They often surrounded him and asked silly questions. Unfortunately, he taught us only for a year. In the late 80s, I started to hear my parents whisper about so-and-so quitting his iron rice bowl job and "going to the sea," which meant someone quitting a stable government job with guaranteed low income and generous benefits and taking on a high risk and high return job or starting his own businesses. Eventually, the seasickness hit the schoolteachers. Our physics teacher quit his job. Some said he went to seek his fortune in Shenzhen, the city in the southern China that established the first economic free zone. I knew my parents wanted me to become either a doctor or a scientist. However, I secretly hope that someday I would become a business owner.

At school, I took part in all kinds of academic competitions: essays, math, physics, and chemistry. I didn't always win first place but I always won something. Each time after the competition, the school would post the winners' names on the blackboard. My name appeared often, so most people in school knew who I was. My father treasured every award I earned, so he made a special folder for me to keep my award certificates. Of course, after each competition, he still insisted on knowing answers to two questions: "Were you in first place?" and "Did you learn not to make the same mistake again?"

In one of the essay contests, we were asked to discuss a Confucius quote: "To go beyond is as wrong as to fall short." Many contestants chose to agree with Confucius because choosing the middle-of-the-road solution and being part of the group is always a preferred choice. I argued from a different angle in my essay: If one has the ability and opportunity to go beyond the rest of the herd, why should one hold oneself back? My Chinese literature teacher told me that she was going to award me the first place, but some other teachers thought my essay showed too much individualist tendency for their liking. So the group voted to give me the second place instead. When I explained to my parents about my second place winning, my father said, "To me, you won the first place, and I am very proud of you." With his encouragement, I became a firm believer in independent thinking.

In the fall of 1989, I started as a freshman in high school. The fall of the Berlin Wall in November received almost no news coverage in China. I was a miserable teenager and was so consumed with my own life that I had little time to care what was going on in the rest of world. I dreaded going to high school because everyone knew that the sole objective of attending high school was preparing for college.

It seemed that China had the tendency to move to extremes. Under the Cultural Revolution, Mao announced that "knowledge is useless," so few people cared about education and many schools were shut down. Now, suddenly the pendulum shifted to the other side, and many people believed that academic achievement was the only path to success. Therefore, anything we teenagers considered fun but the adults viewed as unrelated to any academic achievement was taken out of schools entirely. In high school, there was no more music class or track and field competitions. P.E. class was reduced to a minimum. We never had any homecoming dance parties like American high schools did. I didn't know what I had missed until later, when I lived in America. Like all high schoolers in China, my only responsibility was to spend all my waking hours studying.

In addition to regular classes from Monday to Friday, we had half day school on Saturday. We had a lot of homework, and I rarely went to bed before eleven at night. In addition, we had to take a lot of tests: weekly, monthly, midterm, and final. Parents, teachers, and principals zeroed in on every exam and tried to figure the odds of each of us going to college.

By eleventh grade, we had to choose our majors. Unlike majors in college, for high schoolers, there were only two majors, based on two general career paths. No matter which major we chose, Chinese literature, math, English and political science were considered core curriculum. Major One emphasized heavy doses of chemistry and physics. Students who chose this major were destined to become engineers, mathematicians, computer scientists, etc. Major Two emphasized heavy doses of history, literature, and political science. It supposedly led to college majors such as liberal arts, teaching, journalism, and business.

The whole process of choosing a major that would have a lifelong impact at the age of sixteen or seventeen was very stressful. Like my friends, I dreaded the notion that my choice would pretty much determine my future profession. I learned from my parents' experience that once the decision was made, I would have very little opportunity to change it. That was an enormous responsibility for a sixteen year old. Many students chose Major One because they believed they would gain solid technical skills that would lead to a broader selection of stable and well-paid jobs in a variety of industries. Career choices for Major Two were considerably narrower. A business major was a relatively new concept, so few people knew what it would entail.

Fortunately, I have two older siblings who had to do the same things before me, and they offered me some useful suggestions. My sister chose Major Two when she was in high school, because she really wanted to become a journalist. She realized her dream when I was in eleventh grade and became a reporter for a local newspaper. She loved her job, but the pay was low. My brother chose Major One when he was in high school because he initially wanted to become an engineer, just like my father. My brother was still in college when I was in high school. He started to become more interested in classes offered by the business schools than those offered by the engineering school. He began to talk about international trade and marketing at our dinner table. I didn't fully understand what he was saying, but the new words he used sounded fascinating to me. He secretly told me that he probably would not become an engineer after all. He wanted to work for no one except himself, so he would start his own business someday. He knew that our parents might not approve, so he made me promise not to tell them.

I knew that my parents wanted me to choose Major One. But truth be told, I was inspired by my brother's strong conviction of being a business owner. I grew tired of being constantly poor, and I thought business would be the only way I could get out poverty and have a good life. Even though at that time I didn't have my brother's courage or even thought about being my own boss, I knew that I wanted to someday become a manager of a successful business and make lots of money. My parents were disappointed when I announced that I would choose Major Two only because I wanted to major in business in college. I told my parents that someday I would make over $100,000 a year, which was equivalent to about a one million Chinese yuan. I could tell they didn't take what I said seriously. They thought I was daydreaming. Based on their own experience, they would rather I choose a major that allowed me to learn a solid skill set like they did. They didn't say "yes" or "no" to me immediately. Instead, they took the time to think it through and had several meetings with my teachers. In the end, they gave me the green light. However, they did make sure that I understood that by choosing to go into an unknown territory that they never had experienced, they wouldn't be much help to me. In addition, they made it clear that the bottom line was that I needed to do well in school no matter what major I chose. I greatly appreciated their open-mindedness and effort to treat me like an adult. What they did for me was unusual; most other Chinese parents simply chose their children's majors.

The school reorganized classes based on students' majors. Since most of my friends from the same class chose Major One, I was separated from the people I had known since seventh grade and went to a different class. I didn't know most of my new classmates, so I felt lonely for the next two years. Those first three years in high school were my least favorite period in my adolescence.

At home, I wasn't allowed to read any novels. My TV watching time was limited to 30 minutes per day; I only watched CCTV news. My household chores were reduced to a minimum. My mom fed me the most nutritious food she could get her hands on. Knowing how many of her hopes were embedded in those stews, sometimes I found them hard to swallow. All I did was study, do homework till eleven o'clock at night, and take tests every couple of days.

To understand why there was so much pressure in Chinese high schools, one has to first understand China's College Entrance Exam. In order to qualify to attend any undergraduate colleges in China, all twelfth graders in China had to participate in Gaokao (高考), the National College Entrance Examination (NCEE). NCEE was a purely academic examination. It was offered once a year and normally lasted for three days, from July 7 to July 9. It was cancelled in 1966 at the height of the Cultural Revolution, and was replaced by a new admission policy of political censorship. Youths from the red classes, such as workers, farmers, and soldiers, could go to college as long as they were recommended by local communists. No academic qualification was taken into account. Because the intellectuals who'd taught in the colleges were sent to labor camps, no one was available to examine any academic qualification of these youth anyway. Colleges were jokes in those years and many college graduates didn't learn anything useful.

The NCEE was reinstalled in 1978 and was administered by the Department of Education. Since then, each year, all twelfth grade students in China took the NCEE on the same day and at the same time nationwide. The first two days, students would be tested on core curriculums, and the exams were the same for everyone. For example, students would be tested on Chinese literature in the morning and political science in the afternoon. The next day's schedule would be math in the morning and English in the afternoon. The exams on the third day would be different for students who chose different majors. For Major One students, it would be physics in the morning and chemistry in the afternoon. For Major Two students, it would be history in the morning and geology in the afternoon.

There are several major differences between NCEE and the SAT in the U.S.:

- In China, only twelfth graders can take NCEE; in the U.S, students can start taking SAT in eleventh grade.
- NCEE is offered only once a year. The majority of Chinese students take NCEE only once in their lifetimes. A few of

them go back to twelfth grade for another year if they are dissatisfied with their original exam results and want to try it again. They normally have to endure a lot of humiliation. On the other hand, American students can take SAT multiple times and apply for college based on their best scores.

- Each year, all twelfth grade students in China take NCEE on the same day and at the same time. In the U.S., generally students can choose to take SAT several times a year.

- In China, a student's final total NCEE score is the sole factor that a college considers for admission. In the U.S., a student's SAT score is only one of several factors a college considers.

- In China, the NCEE is not only a test for students, but also a test for parents. The rich and powerful can resort to bribing both high school teachers and college administrators to ensure their children get into a good university. For the rest of us, who have neither money nor power, only the twelfth graders who scored within the top 1/3 on the NCEE will get into colleges on their own. So it is a highly competitive process. This test determines millions of youths' fates forever.

For me, judgment day finally came on July 7, 1992. It was the first day of the three days of National College Entrance Exam. Calculators were not allowed, so we had to do our calculations on a sheet of blank paper. Wuhan was very hot in July. There was no air-conditioning in the classrooms, only a few ceiling fans. I could feel sweat dripping from my forehead. Compared to our parents, though, we couldn't complain. My mother joined other parents in waiting outside the classrooms during each test. They stood for hours under the hot sun with no shade. Many carried water bottles, snacks, and fans. Inside as well as outside the classrooms, we all were tested on our resolve.

By four o'clock in the afternoon on July 9th, the last exam was done, and I was exhausted. I had acne all over my face due to the heat and stress. But the excruciating process was not over yet. Two days later, every university published the minimum NCEE score it required for applicants. Even though we wouldn't know our own NCEE score until two weeks later, we had to fill out a form that listed our preference for universities. Therefore, we had to estimate our scores based on published answer keys.

My college application was a simple form, no essay required. Besides my name and student ID, it asked me to fill out three choices of school. I was told, as a matter of fact, that only the first choice really mattered. Many universities wouldn't accept you even if your score qualified unless they were your first preference on the form. Because we had to choose schools based our own estimated score, not the final score, my parents advised me to be prudent and not to overshoot. I knew for sure that I wanted to go to a college that was far from home, because I wanted some new experiences and to spread my wings a little bit. My father helped me analyze every tier business schools that I qualified for and we finally chose to apply for Tianjin University of Commerce.

People like me, who came from a family with no money or connections, had to depend on test scores. For people who had connections or money or both, many times, they could find someone to sneak their son's or daughter's name to school officials to get preferential treatment. It meant some poor kid would be bumped off the list even if his score qualified him.

I received the admission letter from Tianjin University of Commerce a month later. My time as a high school student was over.

Food for Thought

People often ask me which country has a better public education system, China or the United States. My answer has always been that each education system has its own pros and cons. I wish there was a system that could combine the strengths of both.

For example, one shortcoming of Chinese schools is the tendency to focus more on passive learning and memorization. Chinese schools can learn from American schools by putting more emphasis on teaching students to think, stimulating their creativity and imagination. American schools tend to focus more on making learning a fun process. However, we have to acknowledge that learning isn't always fun. Aristotle said, "The roots of education are bitter, but the fruit is sweet." Some activities, such as memorizing formulae or poetry, are not fun, but are vitally important for students to build a good foundation for learning. Confucius said, "Learning without thought is labor lost; thought without learning is perilous." A good educational system should help students with both learning and thinking.

Everyone knows that for the future growth of America, we need to have educated citizens. As James Madison said, "Knowledge will forever govern ignorance; and a people who mean to be their own governors must arm themselves with the power which knowledge gives." Over the years, a lot of money has been put into education—the U.S. spends on average $12,000 per pupil per year in K-12, one of the highest in the world. Yet U.S. students scored only "average" according to the International Student Assessment (PISA) report. University of Colorado Leeds Business School published a study in 2013 that showed that there is zero relationship between spending and education outcomes. Expensive education reforms such as early childhood education and small class sizes failed to yield consistent and long term impact on student performance.

Education in America is "resource rich and culture poor." It may be time to go back to the basics. Rather than throwing money at it, we need a cultural change. As former Indian president, Abdul Kalam, said, "If a country is to be corruption free and become a nation of beautiful minds, I strongly feel there are three key societal members who can make a difference. They are the father, the mother, and the teacher." A good education system is not simply about how much money it spends, but about dedicated parents, demanding teachers, and committed students.

CHAPTER 13

From Wuhan to Tianjin

Tianjin University of Commerce is located in Tianjin, on the northeast coast of China. It is about 800 miles away from Wuhan. Since my sister and brother went to universities near home in Wuhan, I became the only one to break our family tradition by going to a college far from home. My mom told me that she always knew I would go to some place far away from home because when I first learned to use chopsticks, I always held the far end of the chopsticks. "It was a sign," she insisted.

My going away for college was harder for my mother than for me. I was like a kite that was ready to fly away with excitement. For my mother, it was a bittersweet moment when she realized that it was time to cut the string that held me. She couldn't and certainly wouldn't stop me from pursuing my dreams, but she decided to accompany her baby girl to Tianjin on the first day of school.

We took an all-day train ride from Wuhan to Tianjin. Tianjin is the fourth largest city in China in terms of urban population. Since it sits by the mouth of the Yellow Sea, it has been a major seaport and commerce center in northern China since the 19th century. Just like Wuhan, foreign powers such as the U.S., U.K., and Russia established occupation operations called concessions in Tianjin after the Second Opium War (1858). You can still find Western-style churches and bank buildings in downtown Tianjin. It is also a gateway to China's capital, since Beijing is only about 100 miles away. Tianjin is one of the three special cities (the other two are Beijing and Shanghai) in China that is directly managed by the central government due to its strategic location.

At the train station, the Tianjin University of Commerce set up a reception area. A staff member led my mother and me onto a bus that took students and their families from the train station to campus. We arrived at the campus about half an hour later. Since the university was established by the Department of Commerce in 1980, all buildings on campus seemed relatively new. The campus was not very big, so it didn't take us long to find the school administration office. A staff member there handed me my class and dorm assignments.

Like other universities in China, Tianjin University of Commerce didn't have any co-ed dormitories, so girls and boys lived in separate buildings. There was one girls-only dorm building on campus. It was a six-story building with about twenty rooms on each floor and two restrooms, one at each end of the hallway. Each restroom had two sections: one section was a row of squat-down toilets and another section had a row of faucets and sinks. Only cold water came out of the faucets.

I was assigned to share a room with five other girls on the first floor. Since there was no elevator in the building, I was glad that we didn't have to carry our suitcases upstairs. My dorm room was small, and it was crowded with three bunk beds. The path between them was only wide enough for one person to walk through. There were three holes in the wall serving as storage areas. Despite the room's small size, I had no complaint, because I had been to my sister's dorm room at the Hubei University, and she had to share the same size room with seven other girls in four bunk beds with no storage area. Thus, mine was already an improvement.

My mom picked a lower level bunk bed by the window for me. She put two bottles of homemade pickles by the window. Those were my favorite kind, and I'd had no idea when she packed them into the suitcases. She made the bed for me by covering it with sheets and covers she had made before we had left Wuhan. She also stopped by the campus store and bought me a red thermos bottle to carry hot water. She didn't let me help while she was busy with these details. I guessed they were her way of making sure that I was taken care of when she was not around. I wished she could be around a little longer. But to save money, she didn't spend the night at the hotel. Instead, she rode the night train back to Wuhan. Before she left, all she told me was to study hard and eat well.

For the first time in my life, I didn't live with my family. Instead, I shared a small room with five strangers. It takes a lot of adjustment to live intimately with people you don't know in such a limited space. In addition, the school was run like a military camp. Every night, all lights except two light bulbs in the hallway were cut off at 11 p.m. Given that there was no electrical outlet in any rooms, we had to light candles if we wanted to read or do anything else after 11 p.m. Every morning, all lights were turned on right at six a.m. It was the kind of really bright light, too. I felt bad for the girls who slept on the upper levels of the bunk beds. A deafening speaker on campus started calling everyone to go out running. I secretly wished it would break someday. Unfortunately, it never did. We had to run in the morning every day from Monday to Friday, even in cold winter when the temperature dropped below zero. We couldn't just run wherever we wanted to, either. There was a required route we were supposed to follow. Teachers and student representatives from each class would stand by the gate to punch our cards to make sure that we showed up and ran.

Since the girls' dorm was surrounded by four boys' dorms, we had to walk by the boys' dorms on our way to the cafeteria at least three times a day. There were always boys standing by their balconies to get a good view of the girls. They shouted out scores of how attractive the girls who walked by were. We tried to go to the cafeteria in groups so none of us would be too embarrassed.

My first month of college life started with mandatory military training, which was typical for freshmen in China. Military training was supposedly to help us build character. Each class was assigned two training officers from the local military division, one male and one female. They were probably about the same age that we were. The female officer taught us how to fold our covers in military style and examined the cleanness of our dorms once a week. To win her approval, we had to hide everything inside the storage area before she showed up, even things we used on a daily basis, so our dorm could be spotless. As soon as she left, we brought everything out of the storage area. The kind of tidiness that she demanded was simply unreal. She could be harsh. Once she criticized one of my classmates, who'd forgotten to hide her makeup. The officer threw her makeup into the trash can.

Besides keeping our dorm clean, we had to practice marching like soldiers. Through letters with my friends in other universities, I learned that they had similar military training during their first month of school. Some of them even learned to shoot with real guns. I was kind of jealous of them. We didn't get to touch any guns. Instead, we marched every day under the hot sun. Every day, at least one student would faint. Our training officers dismissed them as the weak ones. Other than marching, the only other thing we could look forward to was patriotism education. We liked it because at least we were allowed to sit down in the playground.

Part of our training was about encouraging us to apply for Communist Party membership. The Communist Party was even more selective than the Youth League. Only past Youth League members were eligible to apply. Those who wanted to become communists didn't have to have the best grades, but their grades had to be above average. Also, applicants needed to have strong recommendations, normally from an existing party member. From the time an application was submitted until it was approved, the applicant had to be on his best behavior, because the Party would closely observe his words and deeds. An applicant needed to demonstrate his steadfast loyalty towards the Party. If the Party asked him to jump, he only asked how high.

I doubt the nineteen- and twenty-year-old people who applied for the Communist Party membership and endured close examinations truly believed the communist ideology. I suspect many were eying better jobs upon graduation, because joining the Party opened the door to unlimited opportunities. At least that was what my roommate Ping told me. She came from a small town in Yunnan province, one of the poorest provinces in southwest China. Her parents were originally from Tianjin but had been sent to Yunnan during Mao's "Up to the mountains and down to the village" campaign. Her parents tried for many years to come back to Tianjin, but were never successful due to the strict household registration system. As a college student, Ping was able to move her household registration from Yunnan to Tianjin for the four years of her education. She desperately wanted to stay in Tianjin and not return to Yunnan.

Ping told me secretly that a Communist Party membership was a sure ticket to a good life in a big city, so she had to apply. She was right. Due to wage control, Communists Party members' salaries were kept about the same level as those of the factory workers', but Party members enjoyed privileged access to many goods and services that were not accessible to ordinary people. For example, Party members enjoyed bigger and better apartments in special apartment buildings in the best locations in the city while paying no or minimum rent. Their children attended special schools with the best teachers. These schools functioned like private schools, so ordinary citizens' children were never eligible. Many of these privileged children went to school in chauffeur-driven cars, not by bus or foot like we did. Party members and their families could shop at special stores that weren't open to the general public. They could get goods such as imported appliances that weren't available to everyone else. No wonder many people wanted to become Party members in spite of the daunting application process.

Ping told me that she had to submit an essay on why she wanted to join the Party. The unspoken rule of this type of essay was to always start with self-criticism. I remembered that Ping wrote many drafts. She tried to strike a balance between listing a modest shortcoming and not undermining her chance. Eventually, she settled on something like that she needed to be more patient. After Ping submitted her application, she was asked to attend secret meetings every other week. She told me that the meetings always started with self-criticism from every participant. I assume that the constant self-criticism in Party meetings was designed to ensure a sense of vulnerability, a sense that no one is above the Party. I was glad I didn't have to put myself through that kind of scrutiny.

When the freshmen military training was over, our classes officially started. One benefit of college over high school was that we had more free time. For most freshmen, since we were new to school and didn't know many people yet, we spent most of our spare time studying. Since our dorm was tiny, we studied in either classrooms or the library. People liked to save their seats by leaving their notebooks on them. That didn't always work, because there were more students than seats available. It was a constant daily struggle to find a seat to do homework and study.

One day, while I was walking around the library to look for an empty seat, I passed a room with a sign that read FOREIGN LANGUAGE PERIODICALS. I pushed open the glass door and walked into a room that smelled of old books. It was a relatively small room with rows and rows of ancient periodicals in English, Russian, and some other languages. There were a few desks and seats available, but they were covered by dust, which meant very few people came here. I liked how quiet it was, so this room became my favorite hiding place.

I didn't know someone was observing me from the moment I walked in. After a couple of weeks, a 50-year-old gentleman came by my desk. He introduced himself as Teacher Hui. Later, I found out that he was more than a teacher; he was the head librarian, who was in charge of this library. The library was his baby. He asked if I could translate a short English article for him, and he offered to pay me. I was more than happy to do it. I didn't want to accept his money when I was done, but he insisted on paying me twenty yuan (about two dollars). I was thrilled; this was the first time I had earned money. From then on, Teacher Hui often asked me to translate English articles for him, and he always paid me handsomely.

As part of the graduation requirement, college students in China were required to pass two levels of National English tests. Students were expected to pass two tests - Level I exam by junior year and Level II exam by senior year. When our English teacher announced this requirement, I asked her if anyone passed the Level I exam as a freshman. She shook her head and told me it had never happened before. I was the kind of person who always liked to ask "why not?" I decided that I would become the first freshman to pass the Level I English exam.

Once I set a goal, I spent most of my waking hours studying English. The vocabulary from our English textbook was obviously not enough, so I began reading the old English periodicals. To help myself with listening, I bought a Walkman that had both a shortwave radio and a cassette player. I cut my food budget and used the money saved to buy books and English cassettes. I even got candles so I could study for one more hour in the dorm after lights off at 11 p.m.

Initially, I bought the walkman to listen to English cassettes. However, by sheer luck, I learned that the AM radio on my walkman could receive programs from the Voice of America (VOA). The VOA is a broadcast organization run by the U.S. government. The quality of reception was poor most times. I had to bring my walkman to different locations in order to find a good area for reception. Finally, I decided that the reception was the best at the small balcony by the end of the hallway. Thereafter, every morning, I brought my breakfast and the walkman to the balcony. I put my earphones on so no one would know what I was listening to, because I didn't want to get into trouble. I knew if I had been caught listening the VOA during the Cultural Revolution, I probably would have been shot to death on the spot. Even though the Chinese government had become more tolerant since then, listening to the VOA was something frowned upon.

When I first started listening to the VOA, my goal was to learn better English. It turned out that I got more than what I bargained for. The VOA opened a whole new world for me. It introduced me to Western cultures and pop music. I was exposed to contemporary rock bands such as U2, Boyz II Men, and Queen. In addition, for the first time in my life, I had an alternative news source. Gradually, I noticed that for the same domestic event, how the Chinese government's mouthpiece, CCTV, reported was different from how the VOA reported.

My efforts paid off. I passed the Level I English exam at the end of the first semester with an excellent grade and became the first freshman in the school's history to accomplish such a feat. Instantly, I became a celebrity on campus.

I kept pushing myself after the initial success. By the end of my second semester, I had passed the Level II exam. Many students considered the Level II exam the most difficult exam of their lives. No freshman had attempted it. The school awarded me a special scholarship and recognized my achievement at the end-of-semester school gathering. My roommates started to imitate me. Every one of them bought a Walkman and lots of candles. When the word got out, girls from other rooms, even other floors, joined the Walkman and candle frenzy. I guess I created a lot of business for the campus store.

Everyone recognized me on campus and everyone wanted me to share my secrets of mastering English, including male students I didn't know. No male, however, was allowed to enter the girls' dorm. A stern old lady sat by the entrance to our building from 6 a.m. to 10 p.m. She would lock the building door at 10 p.m. When a boy wanted to talk to a girl, he had to show this old lady his ID. Then the old lady would call out the girl's name and room number through the intercom system. Since everyone in the building could hear the intercom system, there was no privacy for the girl. Sometimes when boys got tired of going through the old lady, they would stand outside the building and shout out the girl's name and room number. Still, half the building could hear it. My name and room number started to get called out quite often. My roommates wouldn't stop teasing me, and I became quite embarrassed.

In my junior year, the head of school announced that Tianjin University of Commerce had established an exchange relationship with the State University of New York's Delhi Technology College. As a result, we welcomed our first American professor, Professor Reynolds, to our school to teach economics for one semester. Professor Reynolds was a finance professor at Delhi. He looked like the typical American one imagined. He had blue eyes, blond hair, and was taller than almost everyone else on campus.

Professor Reynolds behaved very differently from Chinese professors. Chinese professors were always serious and commanded absolute respect. A class with a Chinese professor meant that we sat there taking notes while he was talking. There was very little interaction. Mr. Reynolds, on the other hand, constantly paced the room and rarely stood still. He treated us with respect, too. He started every request with "Please" and ended it with "Thank you." He never hesitated to say "I am sorry" if he caught himself making a mistake. He was also amazingly honest. When someone asked him if he liked Chinese food, he didn't give the politically correct answer of, "Yes, of course." Instead, he shook his head and said Chinese food was too spicy for him. He missed his mother's pot roast. He rubbed his belly and made us laugh.

Professor Reynolds asked us many open-ended questions to encourage our participation. Most of us weren't used to this kind of interaction, so many of them bent their heads and avoided his blue-eyed gaze. Like Hermione Granger from the Harry Potter series, I became the only student who wasn't afraid to raise my hand to either answer his questions or even ask him a question. Professor Reynolds embraced me more like a friend than a student.

I could tell that Professor Reynolds was homesick, since his life was pretty isolated outside the classroom. Everywhere he went, his interpreter, who was really his guard, made sure he didn't have much contact with Chinese people. Except in the classroom and school-organized tours, he hardly had any opportunity to interact with students. He stayed in a special residence on campus, a two-story building specially designed to house only foreigners. A guard was onsite twenty-four hours a day, seven days a week, and he checked all visitors' IDs.

Mr. Reynolds invited us to visit him a couple of times. We had to sign in at the front desk and were required to leave our student IDs with the guard. We were warned that no visit should be longer than one hour, and we had to sign out when we left. Mr. Reynolds was a good host, though. He played American country music and told us a joke about country music that I remember even today. It goes like this: "What will you get when you play country music backwards? You will get your dog back, your truck back, and your wife back." Professor Reynolds also handed out American candy. I remember that he gave me a Hershey bar. It was the most delicious thing I had ever tasted. I told myself that someday I wanted to go to America to make a lot of money so I could buy lots of Hershey bars.

Professor Reynolds left in May. He must have seen some potential in me, because before he left, he encouraged me to study in America someday, and offered to write a recommendation letter for me. It was the first time someone had told me that studying in America was a possibility. Mr. Reynolds left me his contact information, so we could stay in touch.

In June, we had two visiting students from America. They both were in the MBA program from the University of Washington. Karyn was African American and Marisa was white. I became fast friend with both ladies, especially with Karyn, because she had a daughter who was just a few years younger than me. Even though both ladies stayed in the special residence for foreigners, they moved around more freely than Professor Reynolds had. I wonder if it was because they were women. Anyway, they became the first and only two foreigners who were able to visit my dorm. Since many people had never met a black lady before, everywhere they went, people followed Karyn and wanted to touch her skin to see if it was real. It was good that she never got mad and was always able to laugh it off.

One day, the three of us took a walk to the town outside of campus. While we were walking and talking, a man on the bicycle stopped in front of us. He explained that he was a high school English teacher, but he had never met any foreigners before. He invited us to his home for dinner. Karyn and Marisa were adventurous, so they said yes immediately. They were curious to find out what an ordinary Chinese family looked like. I was worried because if something happened to them, I would be in big trouble, because it might cause some international relationship damage. Neither Karyn nor Marisa had a cell phone with them. Of course, I didn't even know what a cell phone was.

This English teacher lived on the fourth floor of a typical apartment building with no elevator. The hallway was dark and narrow, so we followed the sound of his footsteps. When he opened the door to his home, his daughter and mother sat in front of a small round table. They were surprised to see all of us walk in, especially the two foreigners. The little girl screamed for her mom. Her mom ran out of the kitchen with an apron on. She was a middle-aged woman with a kind face. Her husband introduced us to her and explained to her that he invited us for dinner. She didn't show any displeasure. Instead, she hurried back into the kitchen. She must have been able to do the magic. Very soon, her husband and her mother-in-law brought one dish after another out of kitchen and set them on the little dining table. His room was very small. The three of us sat with him around the dining table. His wife, mother, and daughter sat on small stools. The meal was delicious. Unfortunately, Marisa got violently sick the next day. Whenever we see each other nowadays, we reminiscence about that adventure the three of us shared.

Marisa and Karyn had influenced me greatly. They were both single, but they were financially independent because they were successful business women. Before they started graduate school, Marisa was working in the marketing department of a Fortune 500 company and Karyn owned a consulting business. Because of their professional and financial success, they were able to take time off to pursue graduate studies. They were both hopeful that the knowledge and experience they gained from their graduate studies would make them more competitive and successful in the future. I had never met single and independent women like them, so, naturally, they became my role models. I told myself that, someday, I want to be as successful and confident as they were. Since Marisa and Karyn were still in graduate school when we met, I was able to have a deep discussion with them about the graduate school application process and requirements, and the pros and cons of taking a master's degree right after a bachelor degree. They both encouraged me to apply for a graduate school in America and offered to help in any way they could.

My dealing with Mr. Reynolds, Karyn, and Marisa affirmed my desire to pursue higher education in America. I knew it wouldn't be easy. To apply for graduate schools in America, I first had to take TOEFL and GMAT exams. TOEFL (Test of English as a Foreign Language) measures one's ability to use and understand English at the university level. The GMAT (Graduate Management Admission Test) is an English-based test to assess a person's analytical, writing, quantitative, verbal, and reading skills in preparation for being admitted into a graduate management program, such as an MBA. Marisa sent me a TOEFL preparation book from America that contained practice exams. I didn't do so well on my first try. My friend told me that there were English training camps in Beijing, which could help me to better prepare for those exams. Thus, I told my parents that I wouldn't be home for summer. Instead, I went to Beijing and enrolled into a well-known English summer camp that offered training for TOEFL and GMAT.

It turned out that the training would last for two months, so I needed a place to stay in Beijing. My mother was as resourceful as always. One of her friends' sons, Mr. Wu, was working in Beijing as a high school chemistry teacher. Mr. Wu was able to get an empty dorm room for me. Even though the dorm was far from the English training camp in downtown Beijing, I didn't complain, but rather was thankful that I had a place to stay.

The training camp was run by a bunch of college English teachers. Since they still had their day jobs, they only moonlighted, teaching the camp on evenings and weekends. There was not much teaching, really. Four times a week, I would join other motivated students at a large classroom inside People's University. On the weekends, we would do mockup exams that we were told contained real past exam questions. How they got their hands on them, no one knew. During the weekdays, we would meet three times a week, and the teachers went through and explained exam answers section by section. Then the next weekend, we took another mock exam, and we were supposedly to show some improvement. The teachers tracked everyone's scores, and they were very harsh on those who scored low. They also encouraged us to recite the English dictionary in alphabetical order to increase our vocabulary. I remembered that my father did the same thing when he first learned English. The entertaining moments of those drilling secessions were when the teachers bragged about someone who went through this program in the past and scored very well. Now, they told us, he enjoyed a full-ride scholarship to an Ivy League college in the U.S. This was the kind of role model we were supposed to follow. I felt like a chick squeezed into a chicken farm. There was not much breathing room or anything else except studying and studying more.

I met a girl at the English camp who became a good friend. She told me that she had traveled all the way from Xiamen, a city located in southern China that was thousands of miles away from Beijing. She was an only child, and her parents gave practically everything they had to support her dream of studying abroad. She put a lot of pressure on herself. Every English word she missed during the exam, she would write 10, 20 times until she remembered it. She was my living motivation and closest competition. When not in English camp, I spent most of my time studying in my borrowed dorm.

Finally, it came time to register the real TOEFL and GMAT exams. The cost for TOEFL was $125 and for GMAT was $175. So the total was $300, which was equivalent to 2,500 Chinese yuan. It was more than my parents' ten months' salary. Fortunately, both my sister and my brother worked, so they contributed to my tests fees. On my way to registration, I carried a little black backpack with my wallet inside and hopped on a crowded bus. Before I got off the bus and went to the registration office, someone behind me tapped my shoulder and told me that my backpack was open. I took it down and looked inside. My wallet was gone. Someone must have stolen it on the bus. Somebody might even have seen it happen, but no one had said anything. I started crying because I realized that I had lost my family's savings and my two months' worth of hard work. I didn't know what to do. I went back to the dorm building where I lived and felt my life had been sucked out of me. Mr. Wu happened to see me walk in. My ghostly look alarmed him. Upon his persistent questioning, I told him what had happened. He told me not to worry because he had enough savings that he could lend it to me. It was the money he planned to use for his wedding. I didn't know what to do because it was such a large sum and I had already troubled him so much by living here. I called my sister the same night to ask for her advice. She told me to borrow money from Mr. Wu so I could register for my exams. She promised that she and my brother would figure out how to pay Mr. Wu back and not to tell my parents.

The next day, Mr. Wu got his money from the bank and accompanied me to the exams' registration site. I was able to register for the TOEFL and GMAT on time. Somehow, my parents found out later what had happened. They were proud people and never borrowed money from anyone and always lived within their means. Once again, my family stepped up and paid Mr. Wu back promptly.

After the exams, my friend from the English camp and I decided to celebrate at the McDonald's in downtown Beijing. It was the first McDonald's restaurant opened in China. No one in China knew what fast food was, so there was a long line in front of the counter, and it was difficult to find a table, because people stayed for hours in there. All items were expensive for college students' budgets. My friend and I each bought an apple pie. That was the as close as we could get to something American. It took us a long time to finish eating our small apple pies, because we savored every piece.

I couldn't pursue my dream without my family's support — not only financially, but also emotionally. Telephones were luxuries for many Chinese families. My parents, sister, and brother took turns writing letters to me. I received at least one letter from a family member each week during the three and half years I was in college. Whenever they could, my family came to visit me in Tianjin. My father came most often, due to his frequent business travels. My sister visited me after she graduated from graduate school. She and I traveled to the starting point of the Great Wall and saw the ocean for the first time. My brother visited me after he started working. Normally, a male, unless he was a parent, was not allowed to go inside girls' dormitory. But my brother inherited my father's persuasive speaking skill and good looks. The old lady who guarded the girls' dorm let him in. He did have to leave his ID with her. Still, my brother became the first young guy to visit inside the girls' dorm. All my roommates and the other girls who lived down the hallway tried to flirt with him. I was kind of glad that my school was far from my hometown.

After three months, I finally received my TOEFL and GMAT test scores. I did well enough to qualify for many American schools, so I started applying for MBA programs in the U.S. While I was looking through colleges, my own school — Tianjin University of Commerce (TUC) — made an announcement.

TUC and the State University of New York, Delhi School of Technology, had established an exchange program in 1993. Initially, the program focused on exchanging teachers. In 1995, the universities decided that it was time to exchange students. TUC would select a group of students and send them to SUNY-Delhi for one semester, from January 1996 to May 1996. Participating students would live on campus with American students, take classes like American students, and earn credit towards TUC's bachelor program. Unfortunately, this opportunity came with a hefty price tag. Participating students would have pay $3000 to cover tuition, room, and board for five months, and 15,000 yuan (close to $2000) to cover travel expenses and the expenses for passport and visa. Officially, any junior and senior with a good grade could apply for it, but the final selection would be determined by a group of TUC professors and administrators.

I really wanted to apply for it, but the cost of the program held me back. I knew that my family didn't have that kind of money. Still, I called my father at work from a phone booth to talk to him about it. As soon as I finished, he said, "You should apply." "What about the money?" I asked. He only said, "We will figure it out." We had to hang up quickly to save money. Afterwards, I put my name in the hat.

The selection process was very secretive. No one knew exactly how the finalists were determined. I knew that I should have no problem being selected if the criteria were based on grades and especially grades in English. But like everything else in China, when it was kept a secret, it meant the criteria were not clear cut, so there would be backroom dealings and bribery. I was more concerned about whether my family would come up with that kind of money. My father didn't call me for a couple of weeks. I didn't call him either, because I was afraid to ask. Teacher Hui was on the selection committee, and he mentioned to me secretly that I was selected pending my ability to pay. I thought about it long and hard, then decided that I really couldn't ask this much from my family, so I wrote a letter home and expressed my desire to withdraw my application. Since I had already taken TOEFL and GMAT tests, I could wait to apply for other American Universities and seek scholarships.

Three days after I mailed the letter, I was in my dorm room when I heard the intercom system calling my name. I ran downstairs to the old lady's office. She pointed to the phone on the desk and signaled that I had a phone call. I picked up the phone and heard my dad's voice. He told me that he had received my letter, so he was calling to make sure I didn't withdraw my application. "You are going to America. This is a once-in-a-lifetime opportunity. Don't worry about the money. We will send it in a few days." Dad didn't explain how they got the money. He always kept phone calls short since long-distance calls cost money.

Several days after the phone call, I received a letter from my family. It was a four-page letter. My parents, sister, and brother each wrote a page to express their support for me. My father's page was the most touching. He told me his own story of how he took control of his fate when he left the village for Beijing. He said if I stayed in China, my fate was predictable. The government would give me a mediocre job whether I liked or not. There would be no guarantee that I would go back to live in Wuhan. I could be assigned to some place I didn't like and spend my life there. Very soon, I would be getting married, having a baby, and fighting my husband over how little money we had. "Now, you will be the first person in our neighborhood to go to America. You can shape your own destiny in a way none of us can. Grasp this opportunity and make the most out of it!"

Another week went by after I received the letter. One day, while I was studying in the library, one of my roommates came to find me. She told me that my father was waiting for me in the dorm. I ran back to the dorm and saw my father sitting by my bed. He looked tired. He told me that he happened to have a business trip to Beijing, which was only about two hours train ride to Tianjin, so he had brought the money with him. He had the stacks of money in his well-worn briefcase. He had never had this much money with him before so he hadn't slept all night on the train, worrying that someone might steal it. I accompanied him to see the school administrator. As soon as my father let the school administrator know that we had brought the money, he told us that I was selected. The school administrator took the money from my father and gave him a receipt. We walked out of the office with a light briefcase, but my heart was heavy.

My father didn't stay very long since he had to go back to Beijing for his business. I walked him to the front gate of the school. I wanted to wave a taxi for him, but he said that he would take the bus to the train station. I knew that if he took the bus, he would have to walk a long way to the train station. Since his right leg was injured decades ago in a traffic accident, walking long distances was a challenge for him. But he insisted that the bus was fine and, of course, it was much cheaper than a taxi. While we were waiting for the bus, he told me that to help me realize my dream, my family gave me all the savings they had, including my brother's and sister's savings for their weddings. Even my future sister-in-law contributed her savings. My parents also borrowed money from everyone they knew. My mom kept a notebook in which she had recorded everyone's name and the amount they loaned. It took us five years until I had my first job to pay everyone back, with principal and interest.

My heart was growing heavier minute by minute. The bus finally came and my father patted my shoulder (Chinese people don't hug in public) and said, "I won't come to say goodbye to you before you leave for America. Sending you away is hardest for your mother, so I will let her come, and she will have this final opportunity to say goodbye." I watched him walk towards the bus. He was wearing an old winter coat, and the wind blew through his salt and pepper hair. Tears streamed down my cheeks, and I stood there for a long time.

The day before I took off, my mother and sister traveled all the way from Wuhan to say goodbye to me. They brought two big suitcases with them. One of them was full with homemade beddings and covers. This was only my mother's second time to my school. The last time she came here was with me, when she had helped me settle down as a freshman, and now she came to send me off to an even further place. Her chopstick prediction turned out to be right.

My mother handed me a small bag of money including seventy U.S. dollars, twenty English pounds, and a few Australian dollars. In total, it was less than one hundred dollars' worth of mixed foreign currencies. She told me that this was my pocket money for the next five months, and my brother had managed to get this money for me. At that time, private citizens in China were subjected to a strict foreign currency control. My brother worked at a five-star hotel in Wuhan. Risking being fired, he asked several regular foreign guests who were staying at the hotel to exchange some Chinese yuan into foreign currencies secretly. He offered them better exchange rates than they could get from the bank. To keep the money safe, my mother sewed the moneybag to her undershirt. Now, she transferred the moneybag to me and sewed it to my under shirt. It carried the warmth from her body.

My sister insisted on going out for dinner to celebrate my upcoming new adventure. She and I acted extra dramatic that night. We talked about our trip to the ocean while my mother was mostly quiet. None of us talked much about the trip tomorrow, because we were afraid we would start crying. After my sister paid for the dinner, she showed me her wallet. She had only twenty yuan (less than three dollars) in it. But she patted my shoulder and told me, "Don't worry. It will be full again. You are a worthy investment!"

On the way back to my dorm, we walked by a street vendor who was selling roasted chestnuts. It smelled so good that I asked my mother if we could have some. She shook her head. I knew she wanted to save money, and it didn't bother me at all. As a matter of fact, I soon forgot about this incident. But it tormented my mother after I left China, and she regretted it for many years. Nowadays, she buys me roasted chestnuts whenever I visit my parents in China, even though it is not one of my favorite foods any more.

One of my roommates was a local, so she went home for the night. My mother slept in her bed while my sister and I shared my bed. Nobody slept well.

The next day, my mother, sister, and I got on the bus to Beijing, along with other exchange students and their families. The ride to Beijing was about two hours long, and the road was bumpy. It wasn't a comfortable ride, because the bus was crowded and hot. None of us said anything for a while. I tried to lighten up the atmosphere so I said to my mother, "Ma, when I arrived at America, I will have to eat McDonald's every day. After five months, I would be so fat that you wouldn't recognize me." My sister answered, "In that case, I will be Mom's favorite child." My mother gently stroked both of our hair and said, "You both are my babies and my favorite children, your brother, too." Suddenly, I wanted to cry, and I wanted to tell them that I was scared and I didn't want to go anymore. But I chose to say nothing, just hugged my mother tightly.

When we arrived at Beijing International Airport, my mother and sister helped me to get my luggage checked in. We finally came to a point that they couldn't proceed anymore. I had to go on the rest of the path by myself. We gave one another a final hug. No one said anything, because we knew if someone uttered one word, we would all start crying.

I crossed the line that separated my family and me and kept walking for a few more steps. Before I turned the corner, I looked back. My mother and my sister were still standing there. My sister pulled out her camera and took a picture of me as I waved at them one last time.

Food for Thought

Lao Tzu, an ancient Chinese philosopher, famously said, "A journey of a thousand miles begins with a single step." What he didn't say was that sometimes it is difficult to take that first step. Many of us probably wouldn't do it without strong support from families and friends.

Compared to my parents' generation, I was very fortunate. I met the right people and was in the right place at the right time. Even with all these right elements, I probably wouldn't have been able to change my life without the steadfast support of my family and friends.

There is nothing on earth that I cherish more than family and friends. They are the rocks in my life. They are my source of strength. They enable me to venture into the unknown with great confidence and to be who I want to be.

Valuing families and friends is not something unique in Chinese culture. It is deeply rooted in American culture too. The United States is not a dog-eat-dog world where only the fittest survives. Americans practices self-reliance as a second nature, yet in the meantime, people and community always step in to help one another when there is no "benevolent" government involved—and do so way before any government involvement.

Allow me to share with you a story that always makes my heart tremble. A little over two hundred years ago, a twelve-year-old boy in the West Indies became an orphan. He was dirt poor. His neighbors and local merchants gathered together and took a collection of money. They sent him to go to school in America.

His name was Alexander Hamilton: U.S. Founding Father, chief of staff to General George Washington, Secretary of the Treasury . . . and the face of the ten dollar bill.

CHAPTER 14

There Is a First Time for Everything

I had never flown before until I got on the airplane at the Beijing International Airport. Like many of my fellow exchange students, I was excited to walk into the airplane for the first time. It was big inside and crowded. Everything seemed fascinating and luxurious, even though we sat in the last couple rows in coach section. I touched everything: the armrests, the overhead lights, our own ear-buds, even the pillows and blankets. Some of my fellow exchange students obviously came from well-to-do families and had flown before. One of them handed me a piece of gum and told me to start chewing it to help alleviate ear pressure when the plane took off. He also showed me how to put the safety belt on.

Soon, the engine started to roar. I tried to look outside through the small window. I didn't see much. It was a typical gray winter's day in Beijing. I knew that my mother and sister were out there. I knew they wouldn't leave until my plane took off. The thought of them brought tears to my eyes. Had I known then that I would have to wait five long years before I could see them again, I probably would never set my feet on the plane.

After a 13-hour flight, my excitement of flying was melted by fatigue. We arrived at JFK International Airport at night. It was hard to imagine that now I was on foreign soil. Just hours ago, I had been waving goodbye to my mom and sister.

The State University of New York, Delhi College, sent a small van to pick us up. Perhaps the school staff had never dealt with Chinese travelers before; they were apparently shocked by how much luggage we had.

After loading the luggage, we practically had to sit on top of each other to fit in.

We wanted to see what the world-famous New York City looked like. We imagined lights and skyscrapers. The ride from JFK airport to Delhi was about three hours and didn't pass Manhattan at all. We were disappointed. Soon, many of us dozed off.

By the time we woke up, we had arrived at Russell Hall, a dormitory inside the campus of Delhi Technology College. We helped one another unload the luggage while Teacher Yang worked out the room assignments.

Ying, a short-haired girl, and I would share one room. When we walked into our room, we were wowed. No more bunk beds. Each of us had our own twin bed, a nightstand with a lamp, and a desk. We also had a walk-in closet. None of us ever had one before. I walked in and out of the closet several times, just for the fun of it.

Ying went out of the door to check out other amenities while I was unpacking my luggage. I couldn't wait to hang my clothes in a real walk-in closet for the first time. Ying came back a few minutes later and told me that she had discovered there were a lot of bathrooms on our floor. Basically, every three rooms shared one. I didn't believe her. She dragged me out of the door to see it myself. There was a large bathroom just around corner. It was spacious, well lit, and its porcelain tiles were white like snow. The bathroom seemed very clean and we couldn't smell any odor. There were several porcelain sinks and big mirrors and each toilet had a door. It also had two bathtubs, and each came with a white shower curtain. "Do you know what this means?" I turned to Ying. "We can take shower in private from now on!" No more communal showers. No more sharing a showerhead with a bunch of other naked bodies.

After I finished unpacking, I decided to take a shower. The warm water came out of the showerhead in gentle streams that fell on my face like a mother's hand. The mist wrapped around me like a blanket. It felt very comforting. I started humming my favorite songs. Just at this time, I heard a male's voice. A guy came into the bathroom and started peeing. I froze immediately and didn't know what to do. There was only a shower curtain between him and me. I was terrified that he might walk over and lift the shower curtain. Even though I knew Russell hall was a co-ed dormitory, since I'd never lived in a co-ed dormitory before, I was not prepared for a close encounter with a guy when there was only a shower curtain separating us.

Then the strangest thing happened. He finished his business and walked away. Somehow, this encounter wasn't a big deal to him.

I couldn't comprehend what had happened. I turned off the shower and covered myself as soon as I could and hurried back into my room. Later, I learned what co-ed meant. There was no guard at the front door of our dormitory. Boys and girls not only lived in the same building, they also shared the same floors. They could visit one another any time they wanted and even spend the night in one another's rooms whenever they wanted to. No one cared. There was no mandatory lights on/off time.

I slept well my first night. There was no loudspeaker to wake me up and force me to do morning jogging.

The next morning, we walked together to the cafeteria for breakfast. I hadn't had anything since the last meal on the flight, so I was starving. Breakfast was served as buffet style. I noticed there were only a few hot food items, such as scrambled eggs and bacon. Most other food was cold: cold cereal, cold egg, cold salad, cold yogurt. Growing up in China, I'd always had hot food for breakfast. This was a big adjustment for me.

I fell in love with bacon immediately. It became my favorite food in the cafeteria. Many of my fellow exchange students didn't like the cafeteria food. They found out that there was a Chinese restaurant nearby and learned to order takeout like American students did. I was the only one who didn't follow the trend, because I didn't have much money. I had to preserve my $100 for a rainy day. Therefore, I learned to adjust to American food. Before long, I discovered that blue cheese and honey mustard salad dressing could be quite tasty.

Living on campus in America represented many first-time experiences for me. For example, when I lived in China, we never had fire drills. We never had fire alarms or smoke detectors in our homes and very rarely saw one in public buildings. The first night when we moved into Russell Hall, the RA, Dianna, showed us the nearest exits and pointed out that there was a smoke detector in every room. She emphasized that when the smoke detector went off, everyone must leave the building. None of us took her seriously. One night, I was woken up by the deafening smoke alarm. It was impossible to go back to sleep. I quickly put on my clothes. Then I heard someone knocking on the door. It was Dianna, the RA. She said, "Please hurry up. You need to exit this building as soon as possible."

I put on my coat and shoes and joined a group of students exiting the building. No one appeared to be panicking. When I got outside, I saw some American students wearing only t-shirts and shorts. Some didn't even have their shoes on, and some were covering their bodies with blankets. It was apparent that I wasn't the only one who'd woken up in the middle of the night. Soon, the fire truck came. A couple of firemen ran inside the building. Half an hour later, Dianna came out said it had been a prank and there was no fire danger. Everyone could go inside. I heard someone curse. Similar things happened several times more. But prank or no prank, Dianna took her job seriously, and she wouldn't let anyone stay inside the building. I respected her dedication and appreciated the fact that someone else valued my life.

My first class at Delhi was an interesting experience. It was a marketing class. When I walked into the classroom, I noticed that there was no long table to share. Everyone sat on a chair with a desk arm. Apparently, the seats were not assigned either. You could sit wherever you wanted to. The class was much smaller than those in China. There were probably only 20 students in the classroom. I noticed that there were quite a few older students in the classroom. Some of them well into their 40s or 50s.

The professor who taught the class was a short, stocky guy with a heavy accent. When he walked in, I automatically tried to rise up to greet him like I was supposed to in China, but then I noticed nobody moved. When the professor started talking, I couldn't understand half of what he was saying. He kept mentioning ad examples from the Super Bowl. I didn't know what the Super Bowl was. I wrote down "Super ball" in my notebook. When the class was over, I grabbed an older student who sat next to me and asked her what "Super ball" was. She laughed and crossed out what I had written. Instead, she wrote down "Super Bowl," and explained to me that the Super Bowl is the annual championship game of the National Football League, the highest level of professional American football in the United States. She told me that because the Super Bowl is the most-watched game in America, many companies spend a lot of money to create special advertisements for it. I made a mental note to check at the library later, to see if I could find more information about it.

After the first day of the class, I was shocked to learn how expensive textbooks were. On average, each one cost $80. There was no way I could afford any of them.   Fortunately, I learned that American professors always gave a syllabus at the beginning of the semester that listed which chapters were assigned readings. I borrowed books from my classmates and went to the library. The library had large copy machines and charged 10 cents per page. I would print out the pages of the assigned reading. To save money, I used the zoom function to copy two pages onto one legal-sized paper. That was how I got my reading done.

I initially had a hard time interacting with my American classmates who were the same age I was. I remembered one young American student in my class asked me which movie star I liked. I mentioned Gregory Peck and he gave me a blank stare and asked "Who is that?" Another student, who was about 50 years old, jumped in: "He was a movie star from long time ago. He probably passed away by now." Then he asked me what music I liked to listen to. I mentioned Michael Jackson. Everyone around me laughed. Someone told me that Michael Jackson hadn't made any music for a long time and now he was facing a lawsuit on alleged child sexual abuse. It became obvious that the kind of music I listened to and the type of movies I watched were decades behind what the same aged American were experiencing. I felt there was so much to do for me to catch up. It took me a long time to finally get it that Meat Loaf is a musician, not just another name for pasta.

I loved the school library. It was never crowded, and there was an abundant supply of books, newspaper, magazines, and DVDs. Newspapers and magazines, such as the *Wall Street Journal* and the *Times* magazine, were publications that I had only heard of when I had been in China. At Delhi, I made sure to read them every day. They were the news resources where I learned the famine in North Korea for the very first time. Remembering the similar famine that took place in China before, my belief in socialism started to crack. I also took advantage of the library's movie collection and caught up on some new releases. Tom Cruise quickly replaced Gregory Peck as my favorite movie star.

Soon, it was Chinese New Year. This was the first Chinese New Year I had spent in a faraway land without my family. I missed my family and friends very much. My family continued writing to me every week. Through the letters, I learned my parents had installed a telephone line at home after I left for America. However, since international calls were very expensive, we hadn't talked to each other since I had arrived at Delhi.

One of Chinese fellow exchange students gave me his calling card, which had a few minutes left. I dialed our home number. My father picked up the phone. When I heard his voice, I said "Daddy, it is me." Then, for some reason I didn't understand, I started crying uncontrollably. He became worried and kept asking me what was wrong. I couldn't talk because emotions flooded me and I couldn't run away from them. I cried for several minutes until there was a voice on the line reminding me that the phone card had only one minute left. I finally told him that nothing was wrong. I simply missed them very much. I could hear in the background the sound of firecrackers. He told me to be strong and everyone missed me too.

My five minutes was up. I couldn't hear him anymore. That was the first time as well as the last time I cried over a phone call to my family.

Probably a young heart tends to have a short memory. After living in Delhi for two months, I adjusted to this new environment. I liked the American communication style between teachers and students. All professors treated students with respect. American students were relaxed in the classroom. I got used to some of them walking out of the room in the middle of class and nobody making a fuss about it. Students tended to ask a lot more questions. A class was not just about lectures, it was also about discussions. I actively participated in classroom discussion like other American students. I enjoyed working on group assignments. After not too long, I started to get As for my homework and exams. In addition to studying, I got involved with the campus newspaper. Using my personal pictures and narratives, I helped present a special edition on China. Mr. Reynolds, professor of finance, started calling me a star student. Soon, every professor started addressing me by that nickname.

I fell in love with the town of Delhi. Like everyone else, initially I was disappointed I was not in New York City. I thought every city in America would look like what I saw in movies: shining skyscrapers, fancy cars, and fancy people. Delhi was nothing like that. It was a small town. From one end of the main street, you could walk to the other end in 10 minutes. I liked to take a walk down the main street, breathing in the fragrant aroma of coffee and newly baked bread, checking out decorations in antique shops. There were rows of single-family homes along the street, each home with a different architectural style and color combination, as if it had jumped out of a fairy tale.

There were several churches on this short main street. The entire town was clean and peaceful. People on the street were friendly and greeted everyone, including strangers. Delhi was nothing like what I had imagined an American city would look like, but there was something very American about it. I didn't have much material means, but I felt incredibly secure and free. America was where I belonged. I wanted to stay here.

I renewed my efforts at applying for master's programs in American Universities. Among the professors in Delhi College, I knew Professor Reynolds the best, because he had taught me economics when he visited China in 1994. Professor Reynolds had always been supportive of my pursuit of a graduate program in business. In March, Professor Reynolds told me that SUNY Oneonta had started offering a one-year master's degree in business economics. Oneonta is about an hour from Delhi. As it was a state college, the tuition was very reasonable. Another bonus was that Professor Reynolds had been a guest lecturer there for a year, and he knew the Director of the Master Program, Dr. Lubel, very well. I followed Mr. Reynolds's recommendation and filled out an application to SUNY Oneonta. Professor Reynolds wrote a kind recommendation letter for me.

While I was waiting to hear back on my application, one of my classmates invited me to join the business club. During spring break, the business club members, including me, took a trip to Baltimore. We toured the downtown harbor and the locomotive museum. Several male students in my group were fascinated by the old-fashioned locomotive engine. I didn't understand what the big deal was. When I told them that I had ridden in one of those old-fashioned trains a year before, no one believed me.

My most memorable experience was when we went to a Baltimore Orioles' baseball game. I had never been to an outdoor stadium, not to mention a baseball game. The stadium was huge and well lit. Before the game, everyone rose in the stands and a young lady stood in the center of the field to sing the American national anthem. I noticed that everyone around me, no matter what his skin color was, put his right hand over his heart. Many people sang along quietly until, when the song was close to the end, a big roar of whistles and claps erupted. One of my classmates handed me a wrapped hotdog. He proudly said, "I love beer, hot dogs, and baseball. This is what America is about." I didn't understand much about baseball, but I was deeply touched by the American pride and patriotism around me.

When I came back from Baltimore, I received an admission letter from SUNY Oneonta. I was overjoyed, realizing now that I could not only stay in America but also get an advanced degree. I would become the second person in my family, after my sister, to get a master's degree.

Knowing for sure that I would go to a graduate school in the fall, I started looking for a place to stay in Oneonta for the summer. God lent me another helping hand just when I needed it. A retired Chinese professor, Dr. Lou, came to visit us in May. Dr. Lou was about 70 years old. He was a pilot in the Second World War and left the mainland for Taiwan in 1949. He used to teach at the College of Oneonta. Now, he and his wife lived in a nice house not too far from the SUNY Oneonta campus. When he heard that I was going to attend Oneonta's master's program, he offered to pick me up when it was time to move to Oneonta.

The moving date came quickly. On May 10th, as I was waving goodbye to my classmates and Delhi, I realized that I was completely alone. I was the sole person responsible for my future, and I had the freedom to do whatever I wanted. It was exciting and frightening at the same time.

As promised, Dr. Lou drove me to Oneonta. He asked me if I had a place to stay. He never offered to have me stay in his house, and neither did I want to. My parents always taught me to be appreciative of other people's kindness but to always remain independent. I knew that I needed not only a place to stay, but also a job to make a living. A Chinese restaurant seemed a natural choice. I had heard that Chinese restaurants normally provided their employees a place to stay. My plan was that I could look for a job and a place to stay at the first Chinese restaurant I walked into.

Dr. Lou told me that there were two Chinese restaurants in downtown Oneonta, and he knew the owner of the one called "Little Panda." Dr. Lou took me to see Mr. Zhu, the owner of Little Panda. Mr. Zhu was a middle-aged man from Taiwan. When he learned that I had never worked in a restaurant before, he was hesitant to hire me. I guessed that he eventually agreed to hire me because he didn't want to make Dr. Lou lose face. Mr. Zhu told me that I would start working there immediately. Besides restaurant work, I would teach Chinese reading and writing to his two daughters. In exchange, I would be paid four dollars an hour, and I would stay at Mr. Zhu's house for the time being.

When I lived in China, I seldom set foot in a kitchen. I never learned how to cook. I was also used to a life with routines. Working and living at Little Panda was a whole new experience for me. Mr. Zhu's house was a two-story building with an attic. His house was messy and had only one functioning bathroom. There was often no hot water. My temporary living space was in the attic. A dirty mattress on the floor was my bed. Early in the morning, I would accompany Mr. Zhu to the grocery store to buy food. Then we would go back and pick up his wife and daughters. It seemed either that none of them ate breakfast, or that no one bothered to ask me if I needed breakfast. After we arrived at the restaurant, Mrs. Zhu took their two daughters to school. I started mopping floors and cleaning tables while Mr. Zhu started preparing for lunch hour rush. The restaurant officially opened at 11 a.m. I didn't have a defined job description. I had to do whatever needed to be done. If the phone rang, I had to answer it and take orders. When the order was ready, I needed to pack it into different containers and then into a bag for delivery. Mrs. Zhu normally handled the delivery. I helped cook fried food by doing things such as putting eggrolls in a boiler. If there were any sit-down customers, it was my responsibility to bring them menus and water, take their orders, and deliver their food. Often after one o'clock, when the lunch hour rush had died down, I could finally sit down to have some food. My lunch was whatever leftovers there were from unsold food.

After lunch, I would help Mr. Zhu to prepare for dinner: wash vegetables, make dumplings and spring rolls. By 2:30 p.m., Mrs. Zhu would pick their two daughters from school and bring them to the restaurant. I would tutor them in Chinese reading and writing for a couple of hours. This would allow me to sit down for a while before the dinner rush. When it was dinnertime, the restaurant would become busy again. Even the two daughters would jump in to help. They seemed to be much more proficient than I was. It was not surprising, because this was how they had grown up.

Dinner rush sometimes would last till eight p.m. Then we would have dinner together and afterwards clean up the restaurant. I had never used a vacuum before. One of the daughters had to show me how to use it. Our teacher-student relationship was totally reversed. Besides vacuuming the floor, I had to clean bathrooms. I was embarrassed to walk into the men's bathroom for the first time. Mrs. Zhu told me the restaurant was often subjected to health inspections, so I had to scrub the toilet particularly hard.

By ten p.m., we left together and headed back to the Zhu residence. By the time I climbed to the attic and laid down on the mattress on the floor, I was exhausted. Yet I was blissful at the same time. I knew that this physically demanding work was temporary. I was defining my future one day at a time.

My days went like this for the entire summer until school started in the fall. I realized that Mr. Zhu lived too far from campus. I had to find a different living arrangement. There were a lot of advertisements of rooms for rent at the students' union bulletin board, but I couldn't afford any of them. Thankfully, Dr. Lou extended a helping hand again. He owned a rental property adjacent to the backyard of his residence. It was a two-story single-family home not too far from the bus stop. On the first floor, it

Figure 19. In front of my first apartment.

had a dining room, kitchen, and a small room in between the dining room and kitchen. There were two bedrooms and one bathroom on the second floor. He suggested that if I could find two roommates, I could stay in the small room between the dining room and kitchen. He would only charge me $200 per month. This was a great offer. I tore a page from my notebook and wrote my first English advertisement: Roommates Wanted. I posted it on the Student Union's bulletin board. Soon, two American girls, Jessica and Amy, answered the ad. The three of us became housemates.

I didn't own anything except my two suitcases. Dr. Lou lent me all the basics: a twin bed, a small desk, chair, lamps, and cooking utensils. Since the little room where I stayed had no doors, he put a curtain in front of the bed to give me some privacy. For the first time since summer, I had a semi-normal living arrangement.

Having two American girls as housemates was an interesting experience. Since we split our utility bill, Jessica and Amy had to teach me how to understand our monthly utility statements. Once I understood it, I was always the one to come up with the right amount for each person's share while they were still trying to figure it out on their calculators.

Figure 20. Inside my first apartment

We respected one another's privacy. Although my room was in between the kitchen and dining room, and so was a semi-public area, Jessica and Amy rarely peeked in to see what I was doing. They rarely asked my whereabouts or if I had a boyfriend. They would listen if I wanted to talk to them, but they observed a line really well. Amy sometimes brought her boyfriend back to spend the night. Even though Dr. Lou had specified that no boys were allowed to spend the night at the apartment, neither Jessica nor I bothered to tell him. We agreed without saying it openly that Amy was an adult, and she was capable of making her own judgments.

When school started, I had to cut back my hours at the restaurant. I would come to the restaurant to work for one hour during lunchtime and two hours during dinnertime. The restaurant was located on the bus line, so I could catch the bus on campus. I was always grateful for the restaurant job. It provided me with a place to stay, and allowed me to make a living on my own. Yes, I was paid below the minimum wage, but I had no complaints. I always wonder why in America there is a minimum wage requirement but no minimum skill or experience requirement. My pay was commensurate with the fact that I had zero restaurant work experience. Had Mr. Zhu had to pay the minimum wage and above, he would have hired someone more experienced than me. I would have no means to survive.

Limited hours at the restaurant meant limited income. I still owed half of my tuition and I had monthly rent to cover, so I found two more on-campus jobs: I became a math tutor and a helpdesk staff member at the computer lab. Both jobs paid seven dollars an hour, way higher than the pay of the restaurant job. Every day, I juggled classes and three part-time jobs. I memorized the bus schedule. My classmates were always amazed how quickly I walked from place to place. To me, I had so much to do that time was money. Every day, I felt that I was drinking from the fire hydrant.

One night, when I was walking home from the bus stop after working at the restaurant, I was pondering homework and class preparation for tomorrow. I also felt that all my clothes smelt like Chinese food. I couldn't wait to go home to take them off. I didn't even notice a father and a son coming towards me. The son was dressed in a Superman outfit. He saw me and extended his hand "Trick or treat?" he said. I didn't understand what he was saying, but I suddenly remembered that today was Halloween. It was my first Halloween, but I had been so busy that I'd totally forgotten. I searched my pockets for anything sweet that I could give to the little boy, but I had nothing. I said to him apologetically, "Sorry, I don't have any candy." The little Superman looked at me and looked at his father for a second. I noticed that his father was holding a pumpkin-shaped basket. The little boy ran to his father and picked a candy out of the basket. He ran back towards me and put the candy in my hands. "Here, you can have this one. Happy Halloween," he said. All I could say was "Thank you and happy Halloween to you too!" He and his father walked away. That boy probably never realized that his simple act of kindness warmed my heart.

I suddenly felt very lonely. I wanted to belong to something. I wanted to slow down and not be running from point A to B to C all the time. I remembered that there was a Baptist church by the street corner. The next Sunday, I went to the church. A silver-haired pastor greeted me at the door. He made sure one of the regular church-goers, Janice, helped me find a seat. I had no knowledge of the different sects of Christian churches. I just wanted a place that was well lit, warm, and peaceful. I liked the hymns we sang. The music was so beautiful it felt as if angels were speaking to me. I started to go to church every Sunday. It felt like a true sanctuary. The one-hour service became the only time that I didn't have to worry about work, study, money, and future.

I became friends with Janice. She's a very kind lady. She had four children and her husband was a surgeon. She and her husband traveled to Bangladesh several years in a row on mission trips. She taught local women English while her husband treated patients. Janice was a devoted Christian but had a very unassuming style. She asked me if it was all right for her to visit me during the week. I explained to her about my busy schedule. The next time I met her in church, she gave me a gift: an English/Chinese Bible. I had never read the Bible before. I always wanted to, but there was no way to obtain a copy in China when I was growing up. Like all young people, the more the Chinese government forbade it, the more I wanted to read it. Since I had my own copy, I started to set time aside each day to read a few pages. There was one verse that especially spoke to me, Hebrews 11:1:

Faith is being sure of what we hope for and certain of what we do not see.

Whenever I was down or unsure of my future, I would read this particular verse, which gave me strength to go on. Soon, reading Bible and going to church became an integral part of my life.

The first semester had flown by quickly. I saved enough money to pay the second half tuition so I could receive my transcript. In spite of working three part-times jobs, I still managed to get three As and one B+.

The end of the first semester also meant that Christmas was right around the corner. Holidays were usually the most difficult time to be alone in a strange place. Fortunately, I didn't need to worry about what to do. Karyn, one of the two exchange students I had met in Tianjin, sent me an airline ticket and invited me to her home in Washington D.C. for Christmas. Since there was no airport in Oneonta, I had to fly from Albany, which was about four hours away from Oneonta. Janice volunteered to drive me to Albany and pick me up.

It seemed that every time I encountered a challenge or a difficult situation, there was someone who stood by me and was ready to extend a helping hand. I started to believe they were sent by God. I believe that I am here because it was part of God's plan for me. I was meant to be here even though I didn't fully understand why yet. But I didn't feel alone and helpless any more.

When I came back from Washington, D.C., I told Janice that I wanted to be baptized. Janice and I spent the next couple of months studying the Bible together. We also had a meeting with Pastor Gary. On Easter Sunday in 1997, I stood in the pool with Pastor Gary, in front of the entire church congregation. The pool water was warm, but I couldn't stop trembling. When Pastor Gary lifted my head out of the water, I had an incredibly peaceful feeling.

The master's program I was doing at SUNY Oneonta was a one-year program. It focused on economics. My classmates told me that it was not easy to find a job as an economics major. Many of them planned to apply for a Ph.D. program in economics in order to become college professors. I didn't want to become a college professor. I wanted to work in real businesses. I decided that I needed an MBA. I applied to several MBA programs. Both Texas Christian University and University of Wyoming sent me acceptance letters. The University of Wyoming gave me better financial assistance, so I decided to go to Wyoming after my M.S. program in Oneonta concluded.

I had never been to the American West before. I didn't know much about it except what I saw in John Wayne's western movies. People told me that there was no public transportation in Wyoming. You had to either drive or ride a horse. I knew I wasn't going to ride a horse, so I decided to learn how to drive. I registered for a couple of sessions of driving classes at the local driving school. The first time the coach took me to an empty parking lot to practice, I was very nervous. When he yelled "Stop!" I kept pushing the gas pedal. Fortunately, he pushed the brake from his side. Several lessons later, I became much smoother, and I started to enjoy driving.

When I was in China, I rode either a bicycle or a bus to go any distance. Peddling a bicycle might be faster than walking, but I couldn't go very far. In addition, riding a bicycle was a weather-dependent activity. It was never fun to do it in rain or snow. On the other hand, buses offered very limited schedules and limited destinations. One cannot go wherever one wants whenever one wants. Also, riding buses in China means squeezing into a confined space with many strangers, traveling like sardines. There is nothing like a car to give one the ultimate satisfaction of freedom. When I got into a car, I could go anywhere I wanted whenever I wanted.

I was very happy when I passed my driving test and got a New York driver's license. Since a driver's license is almost equivalent to an ID in America, I felt I was one step closer to becoming an American. Looking around, I couldn't find any car that was cheap enough and still reliable. So I decided to wait until I got to Wyoming to buy a car. Flying to Wyoming cost too much money, so I decided to take the Greyhound bus from Oneonta to Laramie, Wyoming.

In 1997, the internet had just started to become popular, and I embraced this new technology wholeheartedly. I planned my entire trip online. To save money, I decided to skip hotels on the way to Laramie. I was young and I didn't mind sleeping on the bus. Thus, I chose the bus connections with minimum stops and idle time along the way. However, I knew no one in Wyoming, so I had to have a place to stay when I got there. I found a reputable bed and breakfast right next to the UW campus and booked for three nights online. I figured that I would find an apartment within three days of when I got there. It was an ambitious plan. I was fully aware that things might not work out. But I had no other choice. It was better to take a calculated risk than to take no risk at all.

In late August, Janice and her husband took me to the Greyhound bus station. They helped me load my two big suitcases onto the bus. We hugged each other one more time. One piece of valuable advice they gave me was to sit close to the driver at the front of the bus, because sometimes things could get dicey towards the back. When the bus pulled away from the station and I waved goodbye to Janice and her husband, I couldn't help my eyes getting watery. Would I find new friends like them? I opened the Bible in my lap. There I saw that same verse again—Hebrews 11:1: "Faith is being sure of what we hope for and certain of what we do not see."

It was for my first cross-country trip in the U.S. From Oneonta, New York, to Laramie, Wyoming was 1,757 miles, according to MapQuest.com. I rode the Greyhound bus for three days and three nights. I had to change buses twice: once in Chicago; once in Nebraska. But for the majority of the time, I stayed on the bus, sitting right behind the bus driver. The scenery outside the windows changed gradually, from lots of people and buildings to very few people, some cows and horses, vast plains and snow-capped mountains. When the bus dropped me off at the Laramie Greyhound station, I thought I had walked into a John Wayne western movie set. It was a lonely, rusty small building in the middle of wildness. It was not even close to city of Laramie. "What have I done to myself?" I wondered. My heart started to sink. Thank goodness there was a workable payphone inside the bus station. I called the owner of the bed and breakfast where I had a reservation. Half an hour later, the owner showed up in a pickup truck to get me.

From there, things went smoothly. The inn was well kept and close to campus. The inn owners were a nice couple. They gave me good advice on living in Laramie. Yes, they said, I had to have a car. There was no bus here. 20, 30 miles was considered a short distance. Also, the first snow could come as early as October, so I needed to be prepared.

I found an apartment on the third day after I arrived in Laramie. It was only three blocks from campus, and I would share it with three other girls. The two American girls living on the main floor were sisters, and their father owned this place. A Japanese girl and I shared the two bedrooms in the basement. The landlord provided me with some basic furniture, such as a bed and a desk. One of the American girls took me to shop for a used car. I bought a stick shift 1984 Ford Escort Pony for $500. Since I had only learned to drive an automatic car, she had to drive my Pony back to our apartment. The only lesson I got was driving around the block one time with her on my side. Then I was on my own. So I practiced a couple more times and quickly got a hang of it. With a new apartment, new car, and new school, I felt everything falling into place.

For the next two years, my life in Laramie was a blessed one. The University of Wyoming in Laramie has a beautiful campus and amazingly diverse student body. There were about one hundred students from China studying there. In my MBA class, there were two Chinese students, three from Norway, two from Finland and four from America. We were like a mini UN. Every Friday, the International Students' office hosted coffee

Figure 21. Snowshoeing with Dr. Jackson to cut Christmas trees

hour and I would meet students from other countries.

The MBA program offered me a scholarship and graduate assistantship, which were enough to cover my tuition and basic living expenses. I didn't have to work part-time anymore. Instead, I absorbed knowledge like a sponge and enjoyed life as a regular college student.

Figure 22. BBQ hotdogs at an MBA class outing

Among other things, I learned how to snowshoe and barbecue hotdogs. Life was good.

After graduating from UW in 1999, I found a job in Denver, Colorado, working for a subsidiary of Citibank. I chose to work in a field where men outnumbered women. I knew very well that to crack my bamboo ceiling, the only thing I could do was to work twice as hard as everyone else and continue to better myself. While at Citibank, I learned about the Chartered Financial Analyst (CFA) designation, which is considered the gold standard certification of the investment industry. I spent the next three years working toward earning the CFA designation. As the saying goes, "There are no shortcuts to anywhere that is worth going!" To prepare for the exams, I joined a study group. My study buddies were Bill and Tom, and they each owned a private wealth management practice. We not only helped one another with our studies, we also traded our superstitious rituals prior to taking the exams. Bill always slept with his textbooks the night before the exam. I wore the exact same outfit, went to the same restaurant for lunch, and ordered the same food for all three level exams. Bill, Tom, and I all received our CFA designations in 2003. My father told me later that there were fewer than ten people in China who had obtained the CFA designation as of 2003. I became a board member for the CFA Colorado Society, chairing the technology and education committee. 2003

**Figure 23. Board of Directors of the Chartered Financial Analyst
Colorado Society**

was an especially meaningful year for me in another sense too. It was the year I started dating my future husband, Mike Raleigh, a wonderful person and a loyal Nebraska Cornhusker fan.

My CFA designation opened many doors for me to take different career paths. Several years later, I was offered a job with DaimlerChrysler Financial Services in Detroit, so I made my second cross-country trip. That time, I drove a brand new Toyota Corolla for two and a half days, covering 1,268 miles. My coworkers at the bank taught me how to use cruise control right before my trip. What I didn't prepare for was that a car company would prefer its employees to drive its own brand rather than a rival car brand. Some of my new coworkers teased me about my car, so after one year, I sold my Toyota and switched to a Mercedes.

After several years' staying with the auto industry, I moved back to Denver. I missed the crystal clear blue sky, the sunshine, the fresh smell of pine cones, and the sight of snow-capped mountains in the west. Only after moving away did I realize that the American West is the most beautiful place on earth. This was where I want to live for the rest of my life.

Figure 24. Getting married at the Red Rocks Park, Colorado

For my third cross-country trip, I decided to fly. The moving company packed my belongings, which were more than two suitcases' worth, and my bright red Mercedes onto a big truck.

In 2008, I married Mike at the beautiful Red Rocks Park in Colorado after dating him for five years. Mike and I had been set up by a mutual friend. Over the years, I have come to appreciate what a great guy Mike is. He is trustworthy, kind, thoughtful, and incredibly intelligent but unassuming. He knows how to put a big smile on my face, and I can always count on him to give me honest feedback and unconditional support.

After working for various financial services firms for thirteen years, I was ready to strike out on my own. I noticed many people suffered significant financial loss during the recession. But when the economy began to recover, I saw the business opportunity to help people get back on track with sound financial advice.

I am a strong believer in "Wealth is freedom!" Based on my own experience, I trust that individuals can achieve financial freedom if they work hard, save diligently, and invest wisely. With this strong conviction of heart, and confident that I had the experience and expertise to help people achieve the financial freedom they deserve, I set up a purpose-driven business, an investment advisory firm.

Owning a business was a risky move. I asked Mike what if my endeavor failed. Mike looked at me straight into my eyes, his blue eyes calm as a tranquil lake, and said: "That has never cross my mind. I am confident that you will succeed!" He even contributed to the name of this adventure. He told me that his family name, Raleigh, is a Celtic word that means "red meadow." Since red is a good luck color in Chinese culture, this name is perfect for me.

Looking back, my journey from a communist country to a capitalist country is a journey from repression and poverty to freedom and prosperity. I have been asked a lot about why I came here and why I wanted to stay. I knew I wanted to be here when I learned about those magnificent words of the Declaration of Independence, the ones that promise that all men will be guaranteed the unalienable rights of life, liberty, and the pursuit of happiness. This land is your land and this land is my land.

America is called the land of opportunity. To me, that means that I don't leave my destiny to others; I leave it to myself. I take care of my own business and, in doing so, understand that I am the sole person responsible for my happiness. When I strive to be self-reliant, help is on the way when I need it the most.

Food For Thought

Like many first generation immigrants, I came here with next to nothing. With God's grace, other people's kind help, and my own effort and persistence, I realized my American dream—like millions of other immigrants who came before me.

It pains me to hear some people who were born and raised in America either minimize or downright proclaim the death of the American dream. They believe that the more government assistance there is in their lives, the better their lives get, and the happier they become. Yet the opposite turns out to be true.

The year of 2013 happens to be the fifty-year anniversary of President Lyndon Johnson declaring war on poverty. Fifty years and $20 trillion later, America has nothing to show, because the poverty rate has barely changed.

In terms of living standard, many of today's Americans poor liver better than middle class citizens in other countries, with air-conditioned houses, cable TVs, computers, and cars. However, more American poor are less self-sufficient today than they were fifty years ago. Economic mobility hasn't changed in a half-century.

The rising economic tide in this country can't lift all boats because some boats are chained by the welfare system. The well-intentioned welfare system ends up hurting the people it intends to help.

It is true that we don't all share the same circumstance; some of us have better material means than others. Poet Paulo Coelho said: "The circumstances and the environment influence on our lives. But we are the one who are responsible for ourselves." The American dream is never about achieving merely material means. It is about the freedom to pursue one's inner capability to the fullest without constraints from government. This true meaning of the American dream is what gave hopes and conviction to millions of immigrants like me.

Maybe it is time for some Americans to renew their faith in the American dream. The first order of business is to break the chain that tied them to a dependency-inducing welfare system, which has been intentionally and systematically undermining American national characters such as self-reliance.

More than two thousand years ago, Alexander the Great burned his boats upon arrival on the shores of Persia in order to commit his men to victory over the Persians, who far outnumbered the Greeks. Maybe it is time for we Americans to "burn the boat" of welfare dependency. For those who have doubts about the likely outcome, they do not have to look very far. In June 2013, North Carolina cut jobless benefits when its unemployment rate was still at 8.9%. By

November, the unemployment rate had fallen to a five-year low of 7.4%. As George Will said "America is a country where we can get better if we choose to get better."

CHAPTER 15

Becoming an American

People often ask me where I come from. I always answer that I am an American in spirit and I just happened to be born in China. However, it turns out that becoming an American in spirit is much easier than becoming a legal American immigrant. My immigration process was lengthy and costly, yet it was nothing out of the ordinary.

When I first arrived in New York in 1996, I was on a student visa. I remained on the student visa when later I enrolled in the MBA program at the University of Wyoming. Upon my graduation from the University of Wyoming, I applied for a number of jobs like any other college graduate. Except in my case, my job search was narrow because I needed my future employer to sponsor me for a temporary work visa. There are more than a dozen visa categories for temporary workers (see Appendix). Because I have two master degrees, I met the requirements for H1B visa, which is a temporary work visa for skilled workers with at least a college degree. The annual quota for the H1B is only 65,000, and demand always far outstrips the supply. Not many U.S. employers are willing to go through the legal and financial trouble of sponsoring H1B visas for foreign students. Therefore, my career choice was limited.

After numerous rejection letters and emails, I was prepared to go back to China until a Citigroup subsidiary in Denver contacted me. I went through rigorous job interviews and came out on top. Before long, my future boss from the bank called to inform me that I was hired and that my starting salary would be $35,000 per year, which was equivalent to about 288,000 Chinese yuan. Neither my family nor I ever had made that much money before. I was more than ecstatic. My future boss had to wait until I had calmed down before he reminded me that his offer was contingent on my H1B visa petition process. Part of the process was for the company to continue advertising this position for three months. In addition, they had to disclose my salary in the advertisement. This process was called the Labor Certification process. It was required by the Department of Labor in order to show that I hadn't taken a job from a qualified American. Whoever designed this particular piece of regulation certainty didn't bother to take into account H1B visa holders' privacy and sense of humiliation.

Fortunately, my H1B visa application was approved within six months. However, the bank's HR representative and legal counsel advised me not to change jobs within the bank because it might lead to a restart of the Labor Certification process. They also warned against my traveling internationally, because each time I left the U.S. for an overseas trip, I had to make an appointment with the local U.S. consulate to reapply for a visa to reenter the country. There was no guarantee that the local U.S. consulate would grant me a visa even if I provided evidence of employment. Therefore, each of my overseas trips became a headache for my boss because he had to be prepared that I might not come back.

The only place I could travel outside of the U.S. was China. To go anywhere else, I had to worry about applying for a visa to go and applying for a visa to come back. My first trip back to China was in 2000. At that time, the U.S. consulates in China only took visa appointments by phone. Months before I took my trip back to China, my sister started making long distance phone calls from Wuhan to the U.S. Embassy in Beijing to schedule a visa appointment. Since the line was always busy, she had to make dozens of phone calls. Prior to my trip, I had to make copies of my passport and all visa-related paper work dating back to 1996, when I first came to the U.S. as a foreign student. The HR department provided me with a letter addressed to the U.S. Embassy about the kind of work I did and why it was important that I come back to the States. I had to designate a carry-on suitcase for nothing but the paperwork. Upon my arrival in Beijing, I had to wait in line at the U.S. embassy to get my visa application approved before I could visit my family. This process repeated several times throughout the years, and my visa-related paperwork grew more and more.

Since the H1B visa is a non-immigration working visa, it was only good for three years. It could be extended once for another three years. That was what the bank did: it got me an extension for another three years. However, according to the law, if I didn't become an immigrant by the end of this extension period, I had to leave the U.S. because I wouldn't have any legal status. The outdated U.S. immigration policy is driven by concepts of family reunification and birthright citizenship. Since I wasn't born in the U.S. and I wasn't married then, the only way to become a legal immigrant was to have my employer sponsor me for an employment-based Green Card (an ID card attesting to the permanent resident status of an immigrant in the United States). But the bank made it clear to me that it couldn't do that since the sponsorship would be too costly. My friends told me that some other employers might be willing to do it, since I had a good education and a valuable skill set. They were right. Before long, I was recruited by a car company in Detroit. It offered to sponsor me for an employment-based Green Card. I thanked God for once again opening a door for me when I needed it most.

The corporate lawyer of my new employer in Detroit submitted my immigration petition in January, 2005. By late 2008, there was no progress. Every year in between, the corporate lawyer had to file additional forms to keep my legal status. My employer paid a lot of money for their continued services and I filled out scores of paperwork. Being in limbo made it very difficult for me to travel anywhere outside of the U.S. I couldn't even visit family members in China, because there is no visa category or legal term for someone like me who wasn't on H1B visa any longer but was stuck in the Green Card process. The limbo was mainly caused by the bureaucracy and arbitrary immigration cap per country. For Chinese and Indian immigrants, the wait sometimes is as long as a decade.

When I was working in Detroit, I had to do a project between the U.S. subsidiary and the Canadian subsidiary. Therefore, I had to cross the Ambassador Bridge between the United States and Canada on a daily basis. My experience with the U.S. border control and Canadian border control were different as night and day. The Canadians were always easygoing with big smiles on their faces. Their process was always quick. On the U.S. side, there was constantly a long line and the agents were more intense. The process always took a long time. There was one incident that I will never forget. One border control agent, after checking my paperwork for a long time, asked me, "How long do you have the privilege to work in my country?" His words penetrated me like a knife. I went back to my apartment and cried. I felt unwelcome. His words reminded me that no matter how much I felt like an American in my heart, without becoming a legal immigrant, some people would always treat me like as an outsider, suspiciously — in spite of me being a productive member of the society, obeying the laws and paying taxes.

When Mike and I got married in 2008, my employment-based Green Card application still wasn't approved. Our lawyer showed us that the latest update from the immigration office was that they were still processing applications they had received in 2003. Our lawyer's advice was to withdraw my employment-based Green Card application and submit a new Green Card application based on marriage. We followed her advice, but she didn't tell us what a humiliating process it would be.

Several months after we submitted our marriage-based Green Card application, we received a letter from the immigration office that asked us to appear at the immigration office in Centennial, Colorado for a face-to-face interview on a certain date and time. My lawyer said that the main purpose of this interview was to ensure our marriage was not a sham. She suggested we get a day off work and drop everything else to make this appointment, because if we missed it, it could take another several months or even a year before the immigration office would reschedule our appointment. She also suggested we bring everything that could prove our relationship was real, such as emails or letters we sent to each other while we were dating and pictures that showed our trips together. In addition, she described the most likely scenario was that Mike and I would be interviewed separately and under oath. If our answers didn't match, my application would be declined. She even sent us a link to some sample questions from past interviews:

- When did your relationship turn romantic?
- What kind of cake (or other food) did you serve at your wedding?
- Did the bride change clothes for the reception?
- Who gets up first? At what time?
- How many alarm clocks do you set in the morning?

- Do you and/or your spouse attend regular religious services? Where?
- Where do you keep the spare toilet paper?

The intimate level of these questions was unbelievable. My lawyer joked that even she wouldn't be able to answer all questions in spite of having been married for 15 years. I understand the reason behind the interview process was that there were some couples who used marriage as a scam to obtain Green Cards. Still, like all other laws and regulations, this process makes the lives of law-abiding citizens harder. I never imagined that I would have to prove my love for my husband to the federal government.

Since there was no way around it, Mike and I each asked for a day off on the day of the interview. Fortunately, our interview went better than I imagined. Mike and I weren't separated into different rooms. I did show the officers pictures of Mike and me when we were dating and our wedding photo album.

After our interview, we waited but didn't hear any updates. We were planning to spend our honeymoon in China, but I needed a legal status to come back to the U.S. When we called the immigration office's 1-800 customer service number, we only got a recording that asked us to check for updates on the web. But the status on the web never changed. So Mike and I each took another half day off and went to the immigration office in Centennial. We were escorted into a room on the first floor. A couple of agents were sitting behind several windows. We went to sit in front one of them and explained to him our situation. After we presented our paperwork and ID, he checked his computer for a while. Then he and I had the following conversation:

"Ma'am, your case is in transit."

"What do you mean? Is it in the mail?"

"No. It says here that it is between second floor and third floor here in the building. We do not know where it is."

Mike became upset and I started to cry. The agent behind the window showed no emotion. Mike wanted to argue with him, but I pulled him away. I knew that it was no use to argue with the front office agent.

Since we had already booked our trip to China, we asked our lawyer to get me a piece of paper saying my Green Card application was pending.

That paper cost me more than our airline tickets. Once again, I carried a suitcase full of legal documents starting from 1996, when I had been student, and we went on our trip to China.

On our way back, at customs in LAX airport, Mike and I had to stand in two different lines. He was in the line for U.S. citizens and Green Card holders, while I was in the line for everybody else. His line was shorter and moved a lot faster. He went ahead to pick up our luggage. When it was finally my turn to speak to the customs officer, he checked my paperwork and told me to wait in another room. I went into another room and waited alongside some other people. Since cell phones had to be shut off, I couldn't call Mike to let him know where I was. I waited for almost an hour until my name was called. Another immigration officer checked my paperwork. He asked me what my immigration status was. I recounted the entire process of my marriage-based Green Card application. He eventually let me in the U.S. When I walked out of that small room, I saw Mike and several custom agents were pushing and scuffling one another. I heard Mike asking, "Where is my wife? What did you do to her?" I ran to him. He saw me and ran to me too. We shared a long hug in the middle of the airport, as if we had been separated for ages.

After we got back from China, we waited for several more months, and finally I received my Green Card. By then, we had been married for a year. My Green Card was only good for two years from the time we applied. Since we had applied almost a year ago, it had one year remaining before it expired. My lawyer told me that this was expected. The immigration office always gave a conditional approval first for marriage-based Green Cards. A year later, Mike and I appealed to the immigration office to get the condition on my Green Card removed. Once again, we had to prove our marriage was for real. In addition to providing financial records with our names, we had to ask some people we knew to sign a legal affidavit to certify our marriage was real. I had just about had enough of this humiliation and suspicion over my marriage. I told Mike that if there were any more hurdles like this, we should move to China.

Fast forward to 2013. It was the 17th year since I moved to the U.S. The condition on my Green Card was removed.

My immigration saga turned me into a political activist. I joined the movement to push for immigration reform because I didn't want to be a passive observer. Instead, I wanted to be the change I wanted to see. I wanted to participate fully in the political process and get my voice heard. To do that, being a legal resident was not enough. I had to become a citizen so I could vote and have the accompanying rights and responsibilities. Despite all the troubles I went through with my immigration process, I applied for U.S. citizenship.

Several months after I submitted my citizenship application, I received a letter from the immigration office that asked me to appear on X day at X time in X location to do my fingerprints. I am used to the fingerprinting process. It has always been the first step whenever I changed my visa types and legal status in the past: from student visa to H1B visa to Green Card. Not to mention that every time I came back from China, the custom agent at the airport recorded my fingerprints. So the government already had at least a dozen records of my fingerprints. I didn't mind doing it again, but the appointment date on the letter turned out to be a date on which I had a business trip, for which I had already booked my hotel and airplane. Therefore, I had to request for reschedule. According to the letter, I could send my reschedule request only in writing. Thus, I wrote a letter to state my request and mailed it out right away.

A month later, I still hadn't received any reschedule letter. I wrote another letter, including a copy of my first letter. Another month went by. I wrote another letter, including copies of my two previous letters. Three months went by and three letters later, I hadn't received a reschedule letter. I called the immigration office's customer service number. After several attempts, I finally got through the annoying automated system and talked to a customer service agent, a real human being. Once I explained my situation, he told me that there was nothing he could do. He had no access to the scheduling system. All I could do was to wait. The immigration office only communicated with applicants via letters. According to him, next time when the letter asks me to be at X location on X day at X time, I should drop everything to be there.

We are in the age of Amazon, Twitter, and Facebook, but I couldn't make a fingerprinting appointment online and choose a time when I would be available. My only option was to wait for a letter from the federal government. Something is seriously wrong with this picture.

Eventually, I did get a new fingerprinting appointment. Of course, I dropped everything else to make that appointment. A few months after the fingerprinting appointment, I got another letter. This time, I was asked to appear at the immigration office on September 18th for an immigration test and interview. I was given a civic knowledge booklet to study. Mike helped me to get ready. He took a lot of joy quizzing me. "How many U.S. senators are there?" "What's the name of our national anthem?"

At nine a.m. on September 18th, 2013, I walked into the immigration office in Centennial. After I waited for about 40 minutes, my name was called. An agent waved me to follow him to his office. He explained the testing process: all I needed to do was to answer 6 out of 10 questions right in order to pass the test. I answered the first six questions correctly, and the test was over. While he was writing on the paperwork, I said to him: "You know, I came from China, and I can pass any tests." He laughed. Next, he asked me to take an oath and answer some questions from the form in front of him. After that, he smiled to me and said, "Congratulations, Mrs. Raleigh! Your citizenship application is officially approved. We have a swearing-in ceremony this afternoon at 1:30 p.m. Can you make it?" I was totally shocked. When I walked into this building in the morning, I thought I was there only to take a test. I was totally unprepared for things to go smoothly. I could actually be sworn in as a U.S. citizen that very afternoon!

I walked out of building and ran to my car. The first thing I did was cry. I have been waiting for this day for 17 years. I had been used to frustrations, disappointments, delays, and long waiting. Now success came so suddenly, I just lost it for a moment. After a good cry, I realized that it was almost 11 a.m. If I didn't want to go through this important step by myself, I'd better make some phone calls to see who could come at such a short notice. I called Mike first and then several girl friends in town. Afterwards, I stopped by a King Sooper grocery store to pick up a quick lunch. When I walked into the main entrance, there were some small American flags for sale. What a coincidence! I immediately grabbed one.

I went home and changed into my favorite red dress. Then I went back to the immigration building around one p.m. There were a lot of people waiting. They all had big smiles on their faces. We were a diverse group of different ages and different skin colors. I heard different languages being spoken. I kept looking at the door to see if Mike and any of my friends had made it. At 1:30 p.m., an officer came in and announced that all new citizens would go up to the third floor first and family and friends would wait here until someone came to get them later. I joined the other new immigrants walking toward the elevator, wondering if I was going to do this alone. Then I saw Mike walking in, followed by my friends Francoise, Tyler, and Laura. Everyone gave me a hug.

On the third floor, an officer handed each of us a packet, and two ladies from the Daughters of the American Revolution handed each of us a

Figure 25. Becoming an U.S. citizen

small American flag. One of the packets was a yellow envelope marked "The White House." In it was a letter from President Obama. Despite our political differences, his letter was warm and appropriate.

After we took our seats, the director of this branch gave a welcome speech and showed us a short video about what it meant to be an American. After that, everyone's family and friends walked into the room, including Mike and my three friends. The director announced that there were 50 people about to become U.S. citizens today and they represented 47 different counties of origins. He called out each country that was represented, and we stood up one by one. I looked around and couldn't be more proud: here were 50 people with different skin colors, age groups, and languages, who had all had journeys getting here. But we had one thing in common: We all made sacrifices to get here because of our hope for a bright future in the land of the free. No matter how many differences there were in our past, today, we became one. We were all U.S. citizens.

After we all stood, the director led us in the oath:

I hereby declare, on oath, that I absolutely and entirely renounce and abjure all allegiance and fidelity to any foreign prince, potentate, state, or sovereignty, of whom or which I have heretofore been a subject or citizen . . . so help me God.

Mike and my friends were snapping photos of me, while I couldn't stop my tears from streaming down my cheeks. I initially tried to control my emotion. But quickly, I decided to just let it go.

Many memories and emotions flooded to my mind. I saw myself waving goodbye to my mother and sister at the Beijing airport; standing by the greyhound bus station, with two suitcases which were almost as tall as I was; scrubbing toilets of the "Little Panda" Chinese restaurant. I suddenly remembered the Bible verse again—Hebrews 11:1: "Faith is being sure of what we hope for and certain of what we do not see." I was meant to be an American, and it had been my destiny all along.

Becoming an American was a wonderful feeling. Francoise and Tyler threw me a homecoming party. In addition, I received many congratulation messages and gifts. One of the gifts I cherished most was a plate designed by Anne Lowe. The plate says, "Helen Raleigh, Made in China. Now live the American Dreams." What a true statement. The date of September 18, 2013 became one of the most important days in my life. It was the date I came home legally and finally.

Two days after my swearing-in ceremony, my husband Mike asked me if I had registered to vote yet. I told him that I was waiting for someone from the Republican Party to contact me and get me started on some kind of party indoctrination process, like the Youth Pioneer Group did in China. He smiled and told me, "Dear, this is America. We do not have any party indoctrination process. If you want to register as a Republican, all you have to do is to go on the Colorado Secretary of State's website and register. It is that simple." He was right. I spent a few minutes on the website and became a registered Republican.

U.S. citizenship means privileges and responsibilities. I take my responsibilities seriously. The same weekend I became a US citizen, I joined several women to educate voters in Colorado Springs about the upcoming recall election in November.   We walked around a neighborhood in Colorado Springs and knocked on doors.   At one sidewalk, we encountered a grandma and a young mother and her baby daughter in a stroller, a small family of three generations. I asked them if they had voted yet. Both the grandma and the young mother shook their heads. They said, "We don't vote," and waved their hands as if to get rid of a fly. "But why?" I didn't understand and I wasn't going to give up. The young mother just shrugged her shoulders and explained: "I don't like any politicians." At that moment, I felt that I had to say something. "I can understand that you don't like them. But if you don't vote, you basically allow bunch of guys you dislike to continue making decisions you don't like which will impact your and your babies' lives." She didn't say anything. I handed her some literature about the recall and said: "You know, I came from China, and I was never given the opportunity to vote for any officials or representatives. It is such a privilege to be able to vote and to get your voice heard. No matter how you feel about the recall, please vote." She and her mother agreed to read the literature and think about it.

I don't know if the young lady and her mother eventually voted or not. I hope that my words at least made them think. To me, being able to vote is a precious right. People in many parts of the world are fighting with their blood for the right to vote. Voting is more than simply marking a name or a Y/N on the ballot. You are making a personal decision: Whether you want to be captain of your own fate or merely suffer and obey. Charles Bukowski pointed out, "The difference between a democracy and a dictatorship is that in a democracy you vote first and take orders later; in a dictatorship, you don't have to waste your time voting." Thank God that I do not live under a dictatorship any more. I wish some of those Americans who give up their rights of citizenship so easily and carelessly could go through the immigration process and apply for citizenship like I did. Maybe, just maybe, they would learn to appreciate their U.S. citizenship as an amazing gift.

While my legal process of becoming an American is over, my cultural assimilation of becoming an American is ongoing.

I have lived in America for seventeen years. One friend told me that he thought I behaved very much like an American. Then he jokingly said maybe not when he noticed me chewing on a snack made out of seaweed. I know cultural assimilation is a lifelong learning process. Based on my personal experiences, I concluded that one has to go through three stages of the assimilation process:

The first phase is: "You don't know what you don't know." For example, one summer evening, Mike and I were getting ready to grill in our backyard like other American families. He told me that he would like to grill some chicken wings. I went to the grocery store, and it took me quite a while to find a bag of chicken wings, only wings. By the time he was ready to grill and I brought out the well-marinated wings, he asked me where the drumsticks were. I wasn't very happy about his question. I demanded an explanation. "You said that you want chicken wings. Why are you looking for chicken legs now?" My husband said: "Dear, in America, when people say chicken wings, they always mean both the wing and the chicken legs." Oh, now I understand. No wonder every time we went to the Buffalo Wild Wings Restaurant for dinner, they always served us wings and legs. I had thought we were getting a good bargain. Now I knew why.

The second phase is: "You know what you don't know." Another example: When Mike and I were dating, he invited me to me watch *Star Wars* with him one night. I was never a fan of science fiction movies, so I fell asleep during the movie. All I could remember later was the beginning: "In a galaxy far, far away . . ." Mike was in disbelief. I knew many Americans loved *Star Wars*, but it was a mystery to me why. The *Star Wars* movies seemed to me like video games for adults—yet I know that phrases such as the Force, Darth Vader, and quotations from the movies hold special places in the hearts of countless Americans.

Even though I didn't understand Americans' obsession with all things *Star Wars*-related, I knew Mike was a fan, and I wanted to be a good girlfriend. Thus, on Mike's first birthday after we started dating, I bought him a Master Yoda action figure as a birthday present. He was happily surprised when he opened his gift, but what I said next brought him more dismay. I asked him, "How do you like the Judas?" He tried to point out to me that Judas was the one who betrayed Christ according to the Bible, while Yoda was the correct name for the wise Jedi Master of Star Wars. I knew the difference in theory, but somehow these two names just sounded so similar to me that it took me a long time to finally not to call Master

Yoda Master Judas. Nowadays, I intentionally mix them up when I want to annoy him.

Mike and I dated for five years before he finally proposed. I suspect my lack of knowledge and appreciation of *Star Wars* was very much a contributing factor for the belated proposal. After we got married, Mike painstaking explained to me that the *Star Wars* movies have deep influence on many aspect of American culture, so I should at least give them a chance rather than dismiss them. I always take Mike's suggestion seriously, so as part of my American assimilation process, I committed to watching all the *Star Wars* movies and staying awake. I am proud to say that I did it, and I learned to appreciate the lessons that *Star Wars* taught about life and politics. One of my favorite quotes is Han Solo's declaration that "There's no mystical energy field that controls my destiny."

Now I am at the third stage of my assimilation to become American: "You don't know what you know." There are still things that I think I know but I don't. The other day I got a parking ticket because I deposited quarters in the meter close to the rear end of my car, not to the meter close to the front nose my car. I was frustrated with myself, but I recognize that my assimilation process still has a long way to go. I am also aware that an assimilation process is not a one-way street. While I am trying to become an American, my words, my thoughts, and interactions with others have influenced their lives. If America is a big melting pot, I am definitely adding my own spicy flavors.

Food for Thought

I am sharing my own immigration experience as an example to advocate for the immigration reform. Why is it so hard for a well-educated skilled laborer like me to work and live in the U.S.? The U.S. is actually facing a skilled labor shortage. The U.S. government says there are 227,000 open manufacturing jobs that are hard to fill because they require people who are good at math and science. A recent survey found 22% of American businesses say they are ready to hire if they can find the right people.

Foreign students represent a cost-effective skilled labor pool. Many of us came to the U.S. to seek higher education. Many of us received K–12 education in our home country and completed four-year college degrees. Yet the current U.S. immigration process and policies make it very difficult for us to work in the

U.S., not to mention become immigrants.

Why do we currently have over 20 different temporary visa categories for temporary workers, with each category enjoying different rights? For example, Denver's professional hockey team—the Avalanche—could have unlimited number of players from Canada. They would all be on O-1 work visas and not subject to country-of-origin limitations. On the other hand, there is a strict cap on the country of origin for H1B visa holders. The message is loud and clear: The U.S. doesn't want too many scientists and engineers from China and India. This country was founded on the principle of "all men are created equal," but the uneven privileges in visa categories send a different message.

The more visa categories we have, the bigger the bureaucracy we have to deal with, which in turn means higher cost, longer delays, and lower satisfaction. Bureaucracy is inherently anti personal freedom. Instead of creating more and more thinly sliced and diced visa categories, why don't we consolidate them and keep one visa type for all temporary workers? Let the market decide if it needs more engineers, professional athletes, or fruit pickers. Let everyone under this one work visa type enjoy the same privileges.

In a truly free economy, labor should flow freely, just like capital. Arbitrary quotas created by bureaucrats don't reflect economic reality; they only enrich lawyers and bureaucrats while imposing hardships on our lives and making us feel like unwelcome second-class citizens.

Countries such as Canada and Australia are using a skill-based scoring system to select those immigrants who best serve their national interests. Why can't the U.S. adopt a similar merit-based immigration system for highly skilled workers? Why can't the U.S. adopt a similar skill-based scoring system to evaluate legal immigration applications and reward highly educated and highly skilled applicants with higher points?

I am not trying to overly simplify the problems that our immigration system currently faces. However, I do not believe we need to create an even more complex so-called "comprehensive" plan with thousands of pages to tackle our immigration issues either. There are straightforward and market-based solutions available as long as politicians are willing to do what is right and not be led by special interests groups.

For those Americans who think that immigrants will take Americans' jobs, I always like to point to a June 2012 study from the Fiscal Policy Institute:

Immigrants represent 13% of the U.S. population, but account for nearly

20% of small business owners. Immigrant-owned small businesses employed nearly five million Americans in 2010 and generated an estimated $776 billion in revenue, according to the Fiscal Policy Institute.[25]

In other words, a more open immigration policy could result in more jobs for Americans.

Those Americans who believe that immigrants are here to take advantage of America's welfare system seem to forget why their ancestors came to America. Being an immigrant takes courage and a unique character. It is not an easy act, because it means leaving your family and friends behind and taking on great risks to live in a different country with a different culture and a different language. I cannot speak for every immigrant, but I know a lot of immigrants like me make tremendous sacrifices to get here. Many of us share the same goal: to live in a land of free and be the best we can be.

"I am the master of my fate: I am the captain of my soul."

—"Invictus" by William Ernest Henley

---

[25] Geduldig, 2013

CHAPTER 16

Confucius Never Said

My husband Mike likes to say that I was a "little communist" when we first met. I remember our heated political discussion on our first date. I was never a Communist Party member, but I was pretty brainwashed by the general communist ideology even though I had some doubts. Despite my family and my own suffering under the Chinese communist regime, I nevertheless firmly believed that government programs, if done right, were the best means to help people. I was supportive of a government-sanctioned redistribution scheme. Why shouldn't the rich to pay more? Why shouldn't everyone have everything?

I believed that I would never see Mike again after our first date. I wondered what my friend had been thinking by setting us up.

Mike told me later that he thought I had the wrong ideas but I could be changed. It probably helped that he thought I was cute. Mike continued to ask me out. One day, he showed me the most powerful graph in the world — the historical GDP per capita graph based on the research of economist Angus Maddison.

It seems for centuries, whether in West Europe or in China, people's living standard didn't change. Resources were controlled by the ruling class; wealth was distributed by power, favor, or force to a lucky few; the vast majority of the population was barely subsisting. Then a divergence emerged in 1600. The GDP of the West experienced a spike (which coincided perfectly with the birth of free market capitalism in the late eighteenth and nineteenth centuries) while China's GDP per capita remained flat. So the economic gap between these two regions gradually grew wider, to the extent that it became what many economists refer to as the "great divergence." China's GDP growth only came after economic reforms in the later part of 20th century. As a matter of fact, if you look at

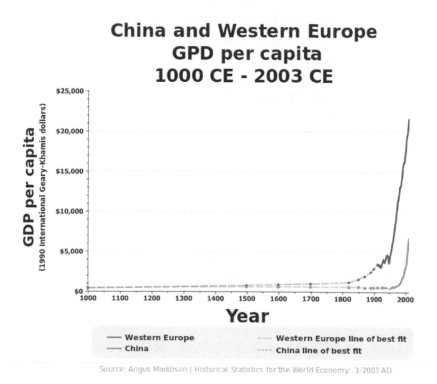

China and Western Europe
GPD per capita
1000 CE - 2003 CE

Source: Angus Maddison | Historical Statistics for the World Economy: 1-2003 AD

other types of historical data, such as population growth and life expectancy, for both regions through the same time period, the graphs almost look identical to the GDP graph. It is not surprising that an increasing living standard brought other benefits such as increased longevity and reduced infant mortality rates. These statistics speak a single message loud and clear: Capitalism works because it is the only system in human history that lifts millions out of poverty. It does the most good for the most vulnerable.

This GDP graph really opened my eyes. Then Mike gradually introduced me to books such as *Free to Choose* by Milton Friedman, *The Road to Serfdom* by Friedrich Hayek, and *Atlas Shrugged* by Ayn Rand. There are some common themes among these intellectual giants, which are the beliefs in individual rights, free market economy, and the rule of law.

They all also denounced tyranny. These readings became my source of enlightenment and transformation. I felt that I was blind before, and these intellectual giants and their books had opened my eyes for the first time.

From 2012 to 2013, encouraged by a good friend, Tyler, I joined the Leadership Program of the Rockies (LPR). I learned how to make a moral case to defend capitalism and eventually became the winner of 2013's "Defender of Capitalism" award.

But more importantly, for the first time, I systematically studied the Declaration of Independence and the US Constitution while attending LPR. I learned what made America great.

America is great because it was founded on the right ideas and a set of timeless and universally accepted principles:

- All men are created equal.
- We are all endowed with certain inalienable rights.
- Self-government by consent.

These founding principles explain why the United States is the wealthiest and most powerful country in the world, and why it is like a magnet, attracting hundreds of thousands of people from every corner of the earth.

Learning these founding principles also got me interested in learning about the founders. I read biographies of Alexander Hamilton, Thomas Jefferson, and Ben Franklin. Through their biographies, I learned that they didn't just come up with these great ideas overnight; rather, they drew on the Western philosophical heritages—from luminaries such as Socrates, Aristotle, Thomas Hobbes, and John Locke.

I love the word "luminary." It gives me the image of the ideas from these intellectual giants being like candles in the darkness, guiding humanity towards a better future.

Did you know before Thomas Jefferson wrote down those famous words in the Declaration of Independence about all men's inalienable rights to life, liberty and pursuit of happiness, John Locke declared that everyone has natural rights to "life, liberty, and property"? As Calvin Coolidge said, "Great ideas do not burst upon the world unannounced. They are reached by a gradual development over a length of time usually proportionate to their importance."

How many people in America today read Socrates and learn about John Locke? The torch of liberty will burn brighter if more of us can spare some time to appreciate the Western intellectual heritage.

A good friend of mine, Bryan, likes to say "Ideas matter." Knowing what make America great also helps explain why civilizations like China, despite their thousands of years' histories, fell so behind in the last two hundred years.

The ideas a society is built upon matter a great deal. For 2000 years, Chinese people followed the moral principles and social orders established by Confucian teaching. Confucius believed that people live their lives within parameters preset by fate. Men should be compassionate towards one another, but there is very little man can do to change his fate. Peace and harmony in society can only be achieved when every man performs his own social responsibility within the preset social orders. Confucius believed people should obey and respect their rulers just as they obey and respect their fathers, while a ruler should love and care for his subjects as if they were his children. Confucius said many good things, but he never said "All men are created equal," because he believed some men were born to be rulers and some men were born to be subjects.

Under Confucius's teaching, the majority of Chinese people endured hundreds and thousands of years' subsistence living; while the ruling class controlled most resources and wealth. For centuries, people could only hope a virtuous ruler would emerge and rescue them from their misery.

When the Communist Party took over China, people thought that Mao was the virtuous leader for whom they had been waiting. His slogan about equality was appealing to the majority of Chinese people. Yet soon, the Chinese people realized the heavy price they had to pay to achieve Mao's version of an egalitarian communist society. His forceful redistribution only ensured that misery was equally distributed among Chinese people; his class warfare eliminated old economic classes but created a new political class system that, in turn, resulted in new class privileges; his thought reform restricted people's ability to think rationally and logically; his destruction of traditional culture and isolation from the outside world erased any point of reference for people; his top-down command and planned economy resulted in famine. Millions of people perished and their voices were never heard; it is difficult to find any traces of them inside the government sanctioned history book. No wonder

Winston Churchill said: "Socialism is a philosophy of failure, the creed of ignorance, and the gospel of envy, its inherent virtue is the equal sharing of misery." Forget about pursuing happiness. People's right to life wasn't even protected.

Friedrich Hayek declared: "A society is built up by the ideas and concepts of people." A society like communist China, which was built upon central planning, where collective will trumps individual rights, cannot compete against a society that was built upon self-governance, individual rights, economic freedom, and rule of law. Real prosperity is only generated by free men. As Milton Friedman pointed out "If you focus on freedom and liberty, prosperity will follow. If you focus on prosperity alone, you will end up losing both prosperity and liberty." Therefore, no one should be surprised to learn that by the 1970s, the average North American was 20 times richer than the average Chinese.

Neither the Confucian teachings nor the Chinese Communist Party's first 30 years' (1949–1979) policies resulted in lifting vast majority of Chinese people out of poverty. Ironically, Mao's brainchild, the Great Leap Forward, was turned into reality only after a limited number of free market reforms took place in China from 1980 onward. Millions of Chinese people lifted themselves out of poverty.

William Easterly, an economics professor at New York University, summarized in his book *The Tyranny of Experts* that "poverty is really about a shortage of rights." Communism failed not because the implementation wasn't stellar enough, but because its policies were driven by the wrong ideas. But a bad idea takes a long time to die. The idea of central planning and forced equality still appeals to many people. When a crisis hit, even some people in the U.S. proclaimed that free market capitalism didn't work and government planning was the only solution. Over the last 30 years, while communist China gradually embraces market economy, the United States moves towards central planning. Policies such as nationalized healthcare, welfare, and minimum-wage laws are destroying real fairness despite their intention, and often end up bringing pain and suffering to the people they are intended to help. Their supporters seem to forget that many aspects of progress in a human society are too complex for conscious planning. They are the "product of human action, not human design."[26]

That is why I feel it is important to share my family stories, which took place decades ago and in a place that is thousands of miles away from the U.S. These stories are relevant today because history tends to repeat itself. Chinese history shows that the erosion of individual freedom is a gradual process, as James Madison observed, "There are more instances of the abridgement of freedom of the people by gradual and silent encroachments by those in power than by violent and sudden usurpations."

Compared to millions of Chinese people, people who are born and raised in the United States are very fortunate. They are born and raised in a society where everyone is free to shape his own destiny, free to live to his full potential. My family's stories are relevant today because the increasing bureaucracies in this country are gradually taking away individuals' decision-making capacities. Bureaucracy is inherently anti personal freedom. You can either accept this situation as it is or accept the responsibility for changing it. Do you really want the government to decide where you can live, what you should learn, whom you should work for, and how many babies you can have?

Silence is consent. Neutrality is not an option. Anyone who wishes to be the master of his own fate and captain of his own soul must, in Ludwig von Mises's words, "Trust himself vigorously into the intellectual battle. None can stand aside with unconcern; the interests of everyone hang on the result."

Someone told me that "Life is a race between education and catastrophes." When you are free to choose, no matter how prudent you are, you will make mistakes and encounter setbacks. That's part of life. Sometimes mistakes and setbacks are the best teachers. They help you build character.

Remember: As long as you have a solid set of virtues and moral principles guiding you like the North Star, you will never get lost in the dark.

---

[26] Adman Ferguson

Appendix

Temporary (Nonimmigrant) Working Visa Categories

Temporary (Nonimmigrant) Worker Classification[27]		
Nonimmigrant Classification for a Temporary Worker	Description	Nonimmigrant Classification for Dependent Spouses and Children of a Temporary Worker
CW-1	CNMI - Only transitional worker	CW-2
E-1	Treaty traders and qualified employees.	E-1[3]
E-2	Treaty investors and qualified employees.	E-2[3]
E-2C	Long-term foreign investors in the CNMI	E-2C
E-3	Certain "specialty occupation" professionals from Australia.	E-3[3]
H-1B	Workers in a specialty occupation and the following sub-	H-4

---

[27] http://www.uscis.gov/working-united-states/temporary-workers/temporary-nonimmigrant-workers

	classifications: **H-1B1** - Free Trade Agreement workers in a specialty occupation from Chile and Singapore. **H-1B2** - Specialty occupations related to Department of Defense Cooperative Research and Development projects or Co-production projects. **H-1B3** - Fashion models of distinguished merit and ability.	
H-1C[2]	Registered nurses working in a health professional shortage area as determined by the US Department of Labor.	**H-4**
H-2A	Temporary or seasonal agricultural workers.	**H-4**
H-2B	Temporary non-agricultural workers.	**H-4**
H-3	Trainees other than medical or academic. This classification also applies to practical training in the education of handicapped children.	**H-4**
I	Representatives of foreign press, radio, film or other foreign information media.	**I**
L-1A	Intracompany transferees in managerial or executive positions.	**L-2**[3]
L-1B	Intracompany transferees in positions utilizing specialized knowledge.	**L-2**[3]
O-1	Persons with extraordinary ability in sciences, arts, education, business, or athletics and motion picture or TV production.	**O-3**
O-2	Persons accompanying solely to	**O-3**

	assist an O-1 nonimmigrant.	
P-1A	Internationally recognized athletes.	P-4
P-1B	Internationally recognized entertainers or members of internationally recognized entertainment groups.	P-4
P-2	Individual performer or part of a group entering to perform under a reciprocal exchange program.	P-4
P-3	Artists or entertainers, either an individual or group, to perform, teach, or coach under a program that is culturally unique.	P-4
Q-1	Persons participating in an international cultural exchange program for the purpose of providing practical training, employment, and to share the history, culture, and traditions of the alien's home country.	Not Applicable
R-1	Religious workers.	R-2
TN	North American Free Trade Agreement (NAFTA) temporary professionals from Mexico and Canada.	TD

Acknowledgements

I'd like to give special thanks to my dear husband, Mike Raleigh, for always encouraging me to pursue my dreams. Sometimes he believes in me more than I believe in myself. His faith in me helps sustain me through many difficult times. Without his encouragement and unconditional support, I could never get this far.

Many thanks also go to two distinguished individuals who I hold in the highest regards: Mr. Lawrence Reed, president of the Foundation for Economic Education (FEE) and Congressman Bob Shaffer. They have been fearless voices of freedom and tireless teachers of free market economics. I owe part of my intellectual awakening to learning from them. I am deeply grateful that both of them took time out of their busy schedules and wrote some very kind words for me.

I also want to thank my two great editors, Bill Brown and Deborah Natelson. Throughout this project, they demonstrated great patience and understanding. They not only helped me polish my writing in English, but also gave me valuable feedback, which constantly pushed me to give my best work.

I want to give my ultimate thanks to my parents, Yukun and Laiying Zhou. They not only gave me the most precious gift in the world — a life — but also made enormous sacrifices so I could live a better life. In addition, they provided a lot of the good material that this book is based on.

Russell Baker said we ought to know that "life is a braided cord of humanity stretching up from time long gone, and that it cannot be defined by the span of a single journey from diaper to shroud." I would like to dedicate this book to my parents, grandparents, great-grandparents, and all my relatives. Their stories were representative of what happened to millions of Chinese people in the first thirty years under the Communist rule. Many of them never had an opportunity to let their voices be heard. Now that my parents are in their 70s, I know that I owe it to them and my ancestors to write down what happened . . . and sincerely hope history will not repeat itself this time.

Works Cited

Canetti, E. (1962). *Crowds and Power.*

Chang, J. a. (2005). *Mao: The Unknown Story.* London: Jonathan Cape.

Commons, W. (2009, 11 05). *Flag of China.* Retrieved 4 11, 2014, from Wikimedia Commons: http://en.wikipedia.org/wiki/Flag_of_China

Geduldig, J. D. (2013, 12 29). *More Immigration Means More Jobs for Americans.* Retrieved 12 29, 2013, from The Wall Street Journal : http://online.wsj.com/news/articles/SB10001424052702303290904579 278173121185300?KEYWORDS=More+immigrants+more+jobs

Giulia, V. (2010, 3 14). *Red Guards (China).* Retrieved 12 3, 2013, from wikipedia: http://en.wikipedia.org/wiki/Red_Guards_(China)

Mao. (1937). *On Practice* (Vol. 1).

Society for Anglo-Chinese Understanding. (n.d.). *Chinese Provinces Map.* Retrieved 1 5, 2014, from Society for Anglo-Chinese Understanding: http://www.sacu.org/provmap.html

Tavernise, J. D. (2012, 2 17). *For Women Under 30, Most Births Occur Outside Marriage.* Retrieved 1 8, 2013, from The New York Times: http://www.nytimes.com/2012/02/18/us/for-women-under-30-most-births-occur-outside-marriage.html?pagewanted=all

Young Pioneers of China. (n.d.). Retrieved from Wikipedia: http://en.wikipedia.org/wiki/Young_Pioneers_of_China

Zhu, J. (2009, 5 13). *Blog.* Retrieved 1 14, 2014, from John-Zhu.com: http://www.john-zhu.com/blog/2009/05/13/the-chinese-education-experience/

Made in the USA
Coppell, TX
08 January 2021

47738670R00132